COMPOSED

THE MOSAIC ADVANTAGE

Leading Without Losing Yourself

THE NEXT EVOLUTION *of* LEADERSHIP
ISN'T CONTROL — IT'S COMPOSURE.

DR. KARISSA THOMAS

Composed: A Mosaic Advantage to Lead Without Losing Yourself

The next evolution of leadership isn't control — it's composure.

COMPOSED: A Mosaic Advantage to Lead Without Losing Yourself

For permission requests, write to:
Mosaic Intelligence Publishing
themosaicleader.com

ISBN: 978-1-968277-50-5

Library of Congress Control Number: 2025925391

Interior Design: Marigold Emal

Printed in the United States of America

The Mosaic Way™, The Mosaic Advantage™, and The Mosaic Intelligence Method™ are trademarks of Dr. Karissa Thomas.

CONTENTS

After the Shock: Learning Composure When Calm No Longer Comes Naturally

Language Cue: Post-Stress Regulation

The process of rebuilding emotional steadiness after acute stress or major life disruption.

> There was a time in my life when staying calm came easily. I thrived under pressure, adapted quickly to change, and carried strength almost automatically. Then, after one life-changing event, everything shifted. The calmness I once relied on disappeared. My body began interpreting even small stresses as danger; my thoughts grew louder, my reactions sharper, and my sense of control weakened.

That was my first encounter with anxiety — not as a personality trait, but as an aftershock. It wasn't constant panic; it was unpredictability. It was learning that even the most capable person can feel destabilized when their nervous system no longer trusts the world to stay steady.

I didn't write '*Composed* from the mountaintop of mastery.' I wrote it from the middle — the space between knowing how to help others stay calm and learning how to find my own footing again. In those years, I discovered what research has since confirmed: emotional regulation after acute stress is not weakness; it's rewiring. Studies from the American Psychological Association and the National Institute of Mental Health show that over 60 percent of adults who experience a major life disruption — loss, trauma, relocation, or identity shift — develop short-term anxiety responses. Most recover. Some remain stuck in vigilance because they never learn how to translate that alertness into awareness.

That's where The Mosaic Way™ started — in that translation. It became my framework for rebuilding composure: through emotional honesty, cultural adaptability, and identity flexibility. Those three skills taught me to listen to my body without shame, to interpret fear as useful information, and to lead with grounded presence even when peace seemed out of reach.

So if you've ever felt thrown off course — not by failure, but simply because life changed too quickly — this book is for you.

You're not broken; you're adjusting. And the truth I've learned is this: composure doesn't mean you never shake. It means you know how to steady yourself again.

A Note on Generations

Throughout this book, generational language is used as a lens—not a label.

Generations are not fixed or uniform categories, but shared social contexts shaped by historical events, technological change, cultural norms, and collective emotional experience. While commonly accepted generational groupings inform this work, they are used here as interpretive frameworks rather than definitive classifications. Individual identity, leadership capacity, and emotional development always extend beyond generational boundaries.

The reflections offered in this book speak less to age and more to leadership posture, emotional inheritance, and the evolving ways individuals and communities define home, work, belonging, and responsibility across time.

This section begins with Generation X, the first cohort to lead amid sustained global disruption, and extends forward to emerging generations whose leadership identities are still forming. The intention is not exhaustive demographic coverage, but continuity—tracing how leadership values, emotional patterns, and adaptive capacity move across generations in response to change.

The Space Between Pressure and Presence

There comes a point in every leader's life when remaining strong no longer works. You continue to show up. You still deliver. But amid deadlines, decisions, and demands, your calm begins to feel like a mask rather than a strength. The people around you see composure; what they don't see is how much emotional effort it takes to maintain it.

I wrote this book for the quiet moments after the meeting ends — when you can finally exhale, but not enough to feel at peace. It's in those small, unguarded pauses that the truth surfaces: leadership isn't about strategy or stamina. It's about emotional integrity — the willingness to stay true to your values when the system around you rewards performance over presence.

The world favors control, but it rarely celebrates composure.

Control stems from scarcity—making you tighten your grip, hurry more, and speak more loudly. In contrast, composure offers something deeper: emotional clarity, attunement, and quiet confidence to lead without losing yourself. It is a practice of grounded awareness, the ability to stay centered even when your environment shifts.

Over the years, I've met thousands of high-performing individuals — including executives, educators, entrepreneurs, and emerging leaders — all asking the same silent question:

How do I stay human while leading through constant change?

That question became the core of *The Mosaic Way*™, a framework built on three key capacities vital to twenty-first-century leadership: emotional integrity, cultural flexibility, and identity agility. Together, they create the foundation of sustainable leadership — the kind that goes beyond self-regulation into relational intelligence, beyond control into connection, and beyond endurance into systemic resilience.

Composed arose naturally from that journey — not another leadership tactic, but a living practice to stay whole in a world that values fragmentation. It invites you to do inner work, develop adaptive capacity, and find the courage to inhabit your identity, even when faced with complexity fully.

If *The Mosaic Way* is about awareness, *Composed* is about embodiment.

It's what happens when your values, emotions, and identity start to move in rhythm — when strength stops being a performance and begins becoming presence. It's the threshold between emotional depth and cultural humility, between reaction and reflection, between urgency and understanding.

This is not a book about perfection or control. It explores a deeper kind of mastery — one that isn't measured by applause or metrics but by your ability to return to yourself after disruption. The kind that allows you to walk into chaos with relational trust, offer clarity without asserting dominance, and lead without sacrificing your sense of belonging.

As you turn these pages, you'll discover stories, reflections, and practical tools that encourage you to pause, listen, and lead in new ways. Each chapter presents a language cue derived from *The Mosaic Way Field Glossary*—a term to help you identify what you feel and handle it with emotional literacy and cultural awareness, because leadership begins the moment you can express what's happening inside you before it influences what happens around you.

You don't need to hold everything together.

You need to become composed — not as a performance, but as a way of being.

The Next Evolution of Leadership

For decades, leadership was seen as a matter of control — over outcomes, people, and oneself. We understood that mastery involved managing emotions, that steadiness meant staying silent, and that vulnerability was a weakness. Calmness became both a currency and a disguise. Over time, composure shifted into performance, and control became a quiet containment.

We learned to project confidence even when our inner world was falling apart under pressure. We perfected the skill of emotional suppression—appearing steady while carrying the invisible burden of uncertainty. For a while, that approach worked. It looked good in a boardroom, sounded competent in a quarterly report, and felt safe in a system built on urgency culture and efficiency bias. But beneath that polished exterior, a crack started to form.

Control began to cost us our connection.

Efficiency started to erode empathy.

Achievement replaced alignment.

And slowly, many of us disappeared behind the image of who we thought we were supposed to be.

The Era of Emotional Noise

We live in an age of acceleration — a world that confuses movement with meaning. Leaders now navigate not only people and projects but also a relentless flow of data, emotion, and decision fatigue.

Technology amplifies everything: urgency, comparison, reaction. It rewards output but rarely values emotional presence.

This is what I call *the era of emotional noise* — the static that builds between what we feel and what we think we're allowed to express. It's not that leaders lack skill; it's that they're drowning in dissonance. The gap between appearance and authenticity has widened into exhaustion.

Real composure, then, is not silence. It's emotional fluency — the ability to identify what you feel, manage how it appears, and express it in a way that fosters psychological safety and relational trust.

Control suppresses emotion.

Composure transforms it.

Control is about holding your breath.

Composure is about remembering to breathe.

From Control to Composure

The next stage of leadership starts where control ends—in the quiet discipline of being whole. Composure isn't about perfection but about being present. It's what happens when your values, emotions, and actions no longer compete for dominance but work together in harmony.

You can't build cultures of belonging with leaders who have silenced their own humanity. You can't spark innovation when emotional burnout replaces curiosity. You can't develop systemic resilience while disconnected from your own inner compass.

Composure is an act of resistance — a rebellion against fragmentation. It's the steady rhythm of grounded awareness in a world addicted to reactivity. When you are composed, you become a stabilizing presence amid volatility. You shift from fear-based decision-making toward values-based leadership.

In a culture obsessed with speed, composure is not passivity. It is deliberate pace — a kind of emotional precision that protects both your energy and your integrity.

The Mosaic Advantage

This book exists because leadership needs a new kind of advantage — one rooted not in dominance, but in integration. I call it The Mosaic Advantage™.

It rests on three interdependent capacities that define the future of leadership:

1. Emotional Integrity — the alignment between what you feel, what you value, and how you lead. It's the foundation of authentic engagement and the antidote to performance fatigue.
2. Cultural Flexibility — the ability to navigate differences with humility and cultural attunement. It means leading across borders, generations, and beliefs without collapsing into defensiveness or distance.
3. Identity Agility — the courage to evolve without erasing yourself, and to hold space for multiple truths within your own becoming.

When these three are in balance, leaders develop adaptive capacity — the inner flexibility to bend without breaking. They achieve what I call composure in motion: the skill to stay grounded while navigating uncertainty, embodying both steadiness and responsiveness.

That is The Mosaic Advantage™ — not perfection, but integration. Not control, but coherence.

Leadership in an Age of Disruption

The last decade has shattered nearly every certainty we've held. Institutions, economies, and identities are all changing. Technology has moved faster than tradition. Workplaces are now multicultural, multigenerational, and geographically spread out. During this shift, leaders are being asked to handle more complexity than ever — emotional, structural, and ethical.

Many admit they are drained — skilled in execution but starved for renewal. They talk about a culture of exhaustion, of clarity hidden beneath chaos, and of an unseen loneliness that no achievement can ease. What they describe is the emotional toll of control — a depletion resulting from constant vigilance and excessive responsibility.

Control drains energy because it resists reality.

Composure restores energy because it aligns with it.

Control is reactive.

Composure is restorative.

When you shift from control to composure, you regain inner sovereignty. You stop reacting to every storm and begin creating your own weather.

The Human Language of Leadership

At the core of composure lies language — the connection between awareness and action. Most leaders are fluent in the language of performance but lack fluency in emotional literacy. They can articulate goals, define metrics, and deliver polished presentations on outcomes, yet struggle to identify what lies beneath the surface of execution. They can explain a key performance indicator (KPI) but stumble over the language of grief, tension, or fatigue. In this gap, emotion becomes noise instead of information, and the human signals that maintain clarity go untranslated. Without emotional insight, stress turns into suppression, and silence leads to separation.

Teams start to function efficiently but relate superficially; conversations turn into reports rather than relationships. The leader's tone hardens, their vocabulary narrows, and their presence loses warmth. Emotional literacy restores that connection—turning composure from a performance of calm into a practice of communication. It provides language for the unseen—subtle shifts in mood, meaning, and motivation—transforming emotion from something to manage into something to understand. Because leadership doesn't begin with what you say; it begins with what you can name.

That's why *Composed* incorporates key terms from *The Mosaic Way Field Glossary*. Each chapter starts with a Language Cue — a concept that helps you understand your internal landscape and express it with relational intelligence. Naming emotion is the first step of regulation; it is how you shift from chaos to clarity.

When leaders develop shared language, they create cultures where people feel seen, not managed — where psychological safety becomes standard, not a privilege. In this way, language isn't just communication; it shapes culture.

The Real Work

Composure is not about being unshakable; it's about being self-aware. It involves pausing before reacting, listening before defending, and grounding before deciding. It doesn't mean you stop feeling frustration or fear — it means those feelings no longer control your leadership.

Every act of composure is an act of self-leadership — a return to integrity in the face of imbalance. It is how we model emotional resilience and create the conditions for collective care. Calm is contagious, but so is panic. Composed leaders influence the emotional climate of their teams not through commands, but through coherence.

This is the real work of leadership today: not doing more, but *being more and not* striving for perfection, but practicing presence.

An Invitation to the Reader

Composed is not a manual; it is a mirror. It invites you to pause, breathe, and realign. Throughout these chapters, you will find reflections, case examples, and daily practices that help you embody The Mosaic Advantage™ in your own leadership rhythm. You'll learn to:

- Recognize when composure turns into performance.
- Restore confidence following emotional exhaustion.
- Lead challenging conversations with compassionate clarity.
- Redefine success by prioritizing values congruence over velocity.

At the end of the book, you'll discover The Seven-Day Practice of Composure — a rhythm of reflection rooted in the emotional and cultural language of The Mosaic Way™. I hope that you finish not only more informed but also more connected — reclaiming the parts of yourself that high performance has caused you to hide.

Because the world doesn't need more control.

It needs more leaders who embody composure.

The Return to Wholeness

There is a calm that doesn't come from silence or retreat, but from alignment — the inner coherence that enables you to lead with both strength and softness. That is the essence of this work. That is *The Mosaic Advantage*™.

Composure is not the absence of emotion; it's emotional wholeness in action — the smooth balance of integrity, flexibility, and agility. It's not about transforming into someone new. It's about recalling who you were before leadership became your armor.

So, take a breath.

Set down what you've been holding just to survive.

And let this be the moment you return — not to control, but to composure.

PART I ———————————————

When Holding It Together Isn't Working

Language Cue: Emotional Fatigue

The unseen exhaustion from maintaining composure for others while quietly falling apart inside.

We don't talk enough about what happens after strength. We celebrate perseverance, grit, and determination — all the words that make exhaustion sound noble — but we rarely explore what occurs when these traits that once made us effective begin to hollow us out.

Many leaders live with this quiet ache. You've learned to read rooms, stabilize chaos, and make decisions while hiding your own uncertainty. People trust you to stay grounded no matter the storm. You've mastered the art of functional resilience — appearing calm while internally fraying. And yet, when the lights dim, you feel the invisible weight of everything you've been holding.

You begin to wonder if you're still leading, or simply surviving.

This isn't burnout in the usual way. You still care. You still perform. But something inside you feels off — as if your body is present, but your spirit has quietly left. That's emotional fatigue — the slow breakdown that happens when emotional restraint takes the place of emotional connection. And it's where many modern leaders start to break apart.

1

The Hidden Cost of Strength

When strength becomes part of your identity, it ceases to be a tool and starts to serve as armor.

You begin to think that composure is your currency, that vulnerability will undermine trust, and that appearing steady is more important than facing the truth of struggle. So, you hold it together — for your team, for your family, for your reputation. You become the emotional anchor for others while quietly losing your own grounded awareness.

But the price of always staying composed is internal dissonance — an unspoken division between what you reveal and what you feel.

Emotions don't disappear because they're managed; they shift. They embed themselves into your tone, your body, your sleep. The tension seeps into small interactions — impatience with coworkers, withdrawal from intimacy, cynicism replacing curiosity.

You find yourself irritated by small things, feeling numb during moments that used to inspire you. Then, quiet self-doubt sets in: *What's wrong with me? Why can't I care as I used to?*

Nothing's wrong with you. You're simply low on emotional resources.

You're relying on borrowed empathy.

The Culture of Endless Capacity

In many organizations, visible control is still valued more than internal coherence.

The system favors those who seem unshakeable under pressure — not necessarily those who practice reflective leadership or psychological flexibility. You're trained to handle crises but not cortisol, to adapt to disruption but not your own depletion.

You develop every type of intelligence — strategic, analytical, operational — except the one that keeps you whole: emotional intelligence with depth. It's not that leaders intend to lose themselves; it's that most have never seen a model of leadership that encourages wholeness. Exhaustion culture becomes the norm. Emotional transparency becomes taboo. And empathy, instead of being the core of connection, is seen as a sign of weakness.

Over time, the system ceases producing leaders who grow — it only produces leaders who simply last. But endurance without growth is merely survival, not genuine leadership. The Mosaic Advantage™ provides an alternative. It encourages you to shift from survival to systemic resilience, from emotional armor to integration. It's not about holding it together — it's about holding yourself as part of the whole.

When Your Calm Starts to Cost You

One common misconception about emotional intelligence is that it always means staying calm. But composure isn't the absence of emotion — it's about integrating it. It's when emotion aligns with your values rather than undermines them.

The problem isn't the pressure itself. It's the disconnect that pressure causes. When you lead without connecting to your emotional core, decision fatigue replaces clear judgment. You start reacting defensively instead of thoughtfully. You talk to people but fail to connect truly.

You solve problems but forget to listen. You lose relational trust, the subtle currency of true leadership. Presence — not position — becomes the real difference between control and calm. Control requires correction: fix, manage, contain. Calm encourages calibration: pause, observe, re-center. Real leadership isn't about who stays unshaken the longest. It's about who remains human most consistently.

Why We Stop Listening to Ourselves

The deepest casualty of constant composure isn't burnout — it's self-betrayal.

You stop hearing the body's early alarms. The tight jaw, restless sleep, and tension that doesn't match the moment — all these signals fade into background noise. You ignore them because stillness feels unsafe.

3

You over-function—staying late, saying yes to everything, filling silence with movement. You mistake visibility for value and busyness for belonging. But movement without reflection causes identity erosion—the gradual loss of clarity about who you are beyond your actions. Machines can sustain output endlessly. Humans cannot. Composure without recovery isn't true composure; it's compression. Its leadership is on borrowed time.

The Mosaic Within

This is where the work begins: not in perfecting performance, but in reclaiming presence. Composure is built through micro-moments of mindfulness — the five-second pause before a reply, the deep breath before a decision, the honest check-in before another yes. These are not small gestures; they are acts of emotional integrity.

When you notice these moments, you begin to see the mosaic within — the intricate pattern of emotion, memory, and identity that shapes your leadership style. It doesn't need to be rearranged; it needs to be integrated.

You cannot lead with integrity if you deny your fatigue.

You cannot model cultural flexibility if you are too rigid to rest.

You cannot embody identity agility if your sense of worth depends on appearing invincible.

Integration begins with honesty. And honesty begins with naming what's real, even when it feels risky. That's why *Composed* starts here — in the exhaustion, in the tension between who you are and who you've been expecting to be, because leadership doesn't begin when you take charge. It begins when you come home to yourself.

Reflection — The First Breath

Before moving forward, take a moment to name your fatigue — not to fix it, but to acknowledge it.

- Where are you acting calm when you're actually over-whelmed?
- Where does feeling in control seem safer than being genuine?
- Where have you mistaken silence for composure?

You don't need to answer aloud. Just breathe them in. Allow your nervous system to recognize it's safe to pause.

This is the first act of collective care — caring for your own humanity so you can lead others without losing yourself. Because the next step in leadership doesn't start with more doing, it begins with one intentional pause — the moment you stop performing and start embodying wholeness.

CHAPTER 1 ———————————————

I See You

Language Cue: Emotional Masking
The deliberate suppression of true emotions to keep up a composed, accepted, or professional appearance.

The Invisibility of Leadership

L eadership today is loud. We are praised for remaining calm under pressure but rarely taught how to stay connected during it. In a world where visibility is valuable, many leaders feel invisible exactly when they are most needed. They stay composed in public but break down in private. This book starts there — in the silent gap between what leaders show and what they truly feel.

There comes a moment in every leader's life when they realize no one has truly seen them in a very long time. You are surrounded by people — meetings, metrics, messages — the choreography of constant coordination, yet you feel strangely invisible. Everyone sees what you do; few see who you are. You've learned to wear calm like a uniform. You smile through strain, listen while your mind races, and deliver clarity when your soul craves connection. Even as your accomplishments multiply, something inside keeps whispering: *But who sees me?*

That quiet ache — the longing to be seen without the need to perform perfection — is where this journey begins. Because leadership without self-awareness becomes a slow decline: the steady drip of authenticity through the cracks of expectation. You can only sustain that stance for so long before your composure starts to cost you your true self.

This is where The Mosaic Way™ begins — the recognition that emotional intelligence is not a trait but a system. A system built on three capacities: emotional integrity, cultural flexibility, and identity agility. When these align, composure becomes connection. When they fracture, leaders begin to disappear behind their calm.

The Burden of Being Unseen

In a global organization navigating a high-stakes merger, an executive retreat took an unexpected turn. The CEO — an astute strategist, composed under pressure — sat quietly at the edge of the U-shaped table as her team debated integration plans. She said little for most of the day. When she finally spoke, her voice trembled — not from fragility but from exhaustion.

"Everyone tells me to be strong for my people," she said softly. "I've been strong for twenty years. Does anyone know what that costs?"

The room fell silent — not the awkward silence of discomfort, but the reverent silence that follows truth. For the first time, her team saw her not as a title but as a human system carrying more than its design allowed.

That moment — though specific — reflects what happens in many rooms around the world. The more prominent a leader's title, the less visible their pain often becomes. The traits that make them effective — composure, consistency, resilience — can also make them distant. They become the person everyone relies on, but no one checks in with.

This is the unseen labor of leadership: emotional containment, relational caretaking, and ongoing self-regulation. These efforts rarely appear in performance metrics or strategic reports, yet they quietly determine whether leaders sustain their purpose or burn out beneath it. Once this labor is named, it can be healed. Naming —

simply allowing truth to surface — is the first act of psychological safety with oneself.

When Calm Becomes a Cage

There is a subtle yet vital difference between being composed and being compressed. Composure is a controlled presence — the calmness that arises from clarity and self-awareness. Compression is silent suffocation — the tightening that occurs when you carry more than your humanity can handle. Both might appear calm on the surface, but their roots could not be more different. One is grounded; the other is neglected.

When your calm becomes a cage, your leadership ceases to be genuine. You start to edit your emotions instead of recognizing them. You replace vulnerability with words — polished phrases meant to reassure others while hiding the truth from yourself. You say, "It's fine," "We're managing," "I've got this," or "We'll figure it out," when what you really mean is, I'm exhausted. I'm overwhelmed. I'm pretending to be strong instead of truly feeling it. You hide behind professionalism because you're afraid of what might fall apart if you pause long enough to feel.

Across sectors — including corporate, educational, nonprofit, medical, and entrepreneurial fields — emotional masking is not just common; it is frequently rewarded. We call it composure. We celebrate it as executive presence. We call it reliability, resilience, and maturity. But often, what we praise isn't true composure — it's suppression. It's the learned ability to hide behind competence. It's the quiet erasure of self in the name of stability. And over time, that erasure becomes costly.

The danger of suppressing calm is that it can be mistaken for excellence. You become the reliable one, the steady one, the unshakeable one — even as your inner world shrinks and tightens. You might feel disconnected from your own needs, your voice, and the people you trust. What started as professionalism turns into an internal exile. You are present in the room but absent from yourself.

This is how calm turns into a cage: when the expectation to hold it together becomes more important than the right to be human, when steadiness becomes a mask instead of a practice. When the people you lead never see the cost of the composure they admire.

Composure is meant to set you free, not trap you. When it turns into confinement, the remedy isn't more silence but greater self-awareness — a return to emotional integrity that recognizes calm is not about suppressing the truth but about steadying it.

The Science of Being Seen

Psychologists refer to this as *emotional attunement* — the ability to perceive and validate another person's inner world. Being seen isn't exposure; it's relational trust in action.

Neuroscience adds another layer. Chronic emotional masking elevates cortisol while suppressing oxytocin — the hormones that regulate trust and empathy. Over time, the body interprets suppression as a threat. You may appear calm, but your nervous system is operating in quiet alarm. The consequence isn't only stress; it's disconnection. Leaders begin to lose access to intuition, empathy, and creativity — the very capacities composure is meant to protect.

When leaders remain unseen for too long, two predictable breakdowns occur. The first is emotional disconnection: you start to distrust your own signals, dismissing exhaustion or minimizing stress until overload feels normal. The second is relational detachment: you project calm rather than connection, signaling distance rather than direction.

The result is cultural contagion. Teams mirror what leaders model. When suppression becomes safety, emotional silence spreads — a subtle form of systemic fatigue that drains innovation and belonging alike.

Visibility, then, isn't about optics; it's about oxygen. When people see a leader embody calm with humanity, they learn that steadiness and kindness can coexist. That is The Mosaic Advantage™ in motion — calm that connects instead of conceals.

Why Leaders Feel Invisible

Leaders rarely intend to hide; they are conditioned to do so. Many grow up in environments where vulnerability is seen as volatility—something to control, downplay, or conceal. In these settings, authenticity still has consequences. Show too much emotion, and you risk being seen as fragile or unprofessional. Show too little, and others may view you as detached or unapproachable. Over time, you learn to navigate the tightrope between sincerity and safety, constantly editing yourself to stay within the boundaries.

But true composure doesn't reside in that corridor. It exists within integration — the expansive inner landscape where your roles, emotions, values, and humanity can coexist without contradiction. Integration shares truths that compression cannot: *I can be calm and still care deeply. I can be decisive and still harbor doubt. I can be strong and still need rest.* When you lead from integration, you no longer must choose between authenticity and stability. You allow both to shape your presence.

Invisibility occurs when leaders begin to confuse emotional containment with emotional erasure. You become so skilled at monitoring your tone, managing your expression, and maintaining a flawless exterior that you gradually lose access to your own inner self. You show up for others in ways that seem grounded, but you stop showing up for yourself. You become a version of yourself that is functional but not full — a silhouette of steadiness that hides the person inside.

Every emotionally aware leader eventually realizes a key truth: you can't be visible to others until you're emotionally visible to yourself. Visibility isn't about performing; it's about building a relationship with your inner world. When you acknowledge your fatigue, hope, uncertainty, and desire for rest — without judgment — you restore safety to your identity. You remind yourself that you can be authentic and fully present without penalty. You stop diluting your presence to meet the expectations around you.

That restoration begins the moment you stop hiding behind your calm. When you allow your steadiness to include your truth —

not replace it — you become visible again, not as the unshakeable leader others want, but as the whole leader your team actually needs.

Mosaic in Action: The CEO Who Finally Paused

During a leadership development intensive, a healthcare CEO admitted she hadn't taken a full day off in three years. "If I stop," she said softly, "the system collapses." Her voice bore the weight of responsibility but also carried the remnants of fear — the idea that rest equals risk.

As part of the program, she was asked to spend just two minutes in silence. No phone. No notes. No planning. No performance. At first, she shifted in her chair, searching for something to do. Then, slowly, the stillness caught up to her. Tears came — not from sadness, but from recognition. "I don't even know what I'm feeling anymore," she whispered.

That moment revealed emotional masking at its peak: a leader so skilled at managing everything that she had lost touch with her own inner world. Without emotional clarity, composure becomes a form of disguise.

Over the following months, she developed what her team later referred to as composure checkpoints — quick moments to reconnect with herself before engaging in challenging conversations or making tough decisions. Each pause focused on three grounding questions:

1. What am I really feeling right now?
2. What does this emotion require — expression, action, or rest?
3. What does composure look like, not as performance, but as presence?

Within weeks, her meetings became more easygoing. Her tone slowed down. Her team started speaking more honestly. What changed wasn't her title or workload; it was her rhythm — the internal shift from urgency to awareness.

That is emotional integrity in action: a calmness that spreads because it's genuine, not staged.

The Language of Recognition

In emotionally intelligent leadership, recognition isn't a reward — it's a relational practice. Genuine recognition goes well beyond achievement. It recognizes the human behind the output, the emotional effort behind professionalism, and the quiet resilience that often doesn't show up in performance reviews.

Most leaders are taught to recognize results, but few are taught to recognize the person. You can praise productivity but still overlook pain. You can celebrate excellence but still miss the exhaustion that created it. You can highlight outcomes, but still fail to see the invisible effort it takes to stay steady under pressure.

Recognition culture transforms the entire dynamic.

It shifts leadership from evaluation to empathy, from metrics to meaning, from performance management to people awareness. Its language sounds different — slower, fuller, more human.

- "I see the effort behind your excellence."
- "I know this transition stretched you, and I appreciate your steadiness."
- "You don't have to prove you belong — you already do."

These are not sentimental statements; they are strategic interventions. They create belonging signals—subtle cues that communicate safety, value, and acceptance of full humanity. Without these signals, teams tend to protect themselves. With them, teams become open, collaborative, and trusting.

Research across industries continues to confirm what cultures of care have always known: psychological safety — not pay, perks, or policy — is the strongest predictor of sustained performance. When people feel seen, they contribute more authentically. When they feel recognized, they offer their best without fear of punishment or perfection.

Recognition roots people in a sense of belonging. And belonging, not busyness, is what sustains excellence. It steadies the nervous system, calms the emotional climate, and transforms teams into communities.

In *The Mosaic Way*™, this is not a soft skill — it's a structural one. Recognition is the language that shapes the culture you aim to lead.

The Inner Mirror

"I see you" is not just a gift you offer others; it is a discipline you practice with yourself.

Before every pivotal meeting, high-stakes moment, or difficult conversation, the first task of leadership is inward. Look toward your own interior — literally in the mirror or figuratively through awareness — and ask a simple but revealing question:

What do I see right now?

Do you notice tension tightening your breath?
Do you feel fear disguised as over-preparation?
Do you sense focus or fatigue?
Is your presence authentic, or are you slipping into performance?
You are not attempting to fix anything.
You are trying to observe what already exists.

Unseen emotions never stay hidden. What you refuse to acknowledge privately will surface publicly — through tone, timing, reactivity, or subtle withdrawal. If you don't name your fear, it will reappear as control. If you don't name your overwhelm, it will express itself as irritation. If you don't name your loneliness, it may show up as over-functioning — doing more, carrying more, proving more.

This is why self-attunement is the key to composure.

Without genuine inner awareness, calmness is just superficial — a display of steadiness instead of an authentic expression.

Composed leaders do not silence their inner world; they listen to it. They treat their emotions not as threats but as information.

They understand that clarity begins with witnessing, and witnessing begins with presence. When you are emotionally visible to yourself, you stop hiding behind professionalism and start leading from coherence.

The Inner Mirror is a calm practice that keeps your leadership authentic. It reminds you that composure isn't the absence of emotion — it's the alignment of emotion, awareness, and intention.

Leadership Reframed: The New Visibility

For generations, leadership was based on projection — the display of confidence, the appearance of certainty, and the posture of command. Strength was judged by how smoothly you could hide strain and how convincingly you could show composure. But projection without reflection leads to distortion. It reveals the role, not the person. It conveys authority, but not necessarily truth.

Today's leaders are influenced by a new vocabulary — one rooted in emotional resonance, cultural sensitivity, and alignment with core values. This change isn't superficial; it's fundamental. The world no longer values leaders who seem untouchable. It rewards leaders who are attuned, self-aware, and able to navigate nuance. In this era, visibility isn't about the spotlight but about presence — the courage to show up with clarity rather than performance.

Authentic composure does not hide emotion; it aligns with it. It doesn't broadcast certainty but shows coherence. It turns openness into trust by demonstrating that steadiness and sincerity can coexist. When a leader says, "I'm not fine, but I'm still capable," they model humanity that strengthens the collective rather than weakens it. They reveal that vulnerability is not volatility — it is visibility. The kind that invites accountability, honesty, and courage from those around them.

In this reframed model, leadership isn't about solitary endurance; it's about shared clarity. When a leader is willing to be authentic in public, it encourages others to follow. It creates a culture of collective care — a space where people feel safe telling the truth, asking for help, and showing their whole selves. As belonging deepens, performance gets better. When humanity is respected, trust grows.

This is the new face of leadership: not louder, but more aligned; not polished, but authentic. It is leadership as coherence — the quiet strength of being genuine, steady, and whole in a world that often expects the opposite.

Reflection — Seeing Yourself Again

Before you move to the next chapter, pause for a private check-in. Ask yourself:

- What am I hiding that no one notices?
- What am I pretending not to feel in the name of professionalism?
- Who truly sees me — and what might change if I let them in?

Leadership that heals begins here — in visibility, in truth, in the reclamation of your full humanity.

Because composure is not the absence of emotion.

It is the courageous integration of what is real.

And it begins with three simple, sacred words:

I see you.

!

The Data That Demands Attention

The numbers reveal what many have quietly carried.

In a 2024 Deloitte survey, 70 percent of professionals reported feeling "emotionally depleted" at least once a week. The American Psychological Association found that two out of three workers identify chronic stress as a direct barrier to performance.

Among leaders, 42 percent admit they conceal their exhaustion to maintain their composure in front of their teams.

Emotional containment has become a silent crisis in leadership. The impact is clear: Gallup's 2023 "State of the Global Workplace" report estimated that unaddressed emotional fatigue costs $8.8 trillion in lost productivity globally.

Maintaining composure is no longer a soft skill—it's a proven factor for retention, trust, and organizational health.

When we talk about "being everyone's calm," we refer to invisible work that supports systems. Recognizing this work is the first step toward repair.

A Word to the Generations

 **Generation X** You were shaped in an era of self-reliance. Strength meant never revealing strain. But the next level of leadership calls for transparency. Let your steadiness include your story.

 **Millennials** You have built bridges through both empathy and burnout. You understand the price of caring without boundaries. Your task now is to lead with rhythm—modeling both drive and recovery.

 **Generation Z** You feel deeply and speak directly. The world often misinterprets honesty as volatility. Protect your sensitivity as an advantage; let composure sharpen, not suppress, your truth.

 **Generation Alpha** You will inherit speed as your default. Remember that presence remains a superpower. The calm you cultivate will one day steady the world you create.

 **Generation Beta** You will enter a world already loud with data. Your first strength will be knowing when you are seen—and when you need to see yourself without an audience.

Which part of your generational voice feels strongest right now—clarity, connection, speed, or listening?

The Composed Practice

Composed — Chapter 1: I See You

Recognition · Visibility · Permission to Breathe

I am not invisible in my strength.
What I hold for others, I now have for myself.
I can be calm and still be seen.

Close the book for a moment.
Let the quiet find you before you rush to the next thing.
Notice how your shoulders feel when you stop performing
    and simply allow it.

You have been the steady one—the one who makes
    composure look effortless.
But even the strong need to be witnessed.
Ask yourself: *Who sees me when I am not holding the room*
    together?
This question is not self-pity; it is self-permission.

Place one hand over your heart and whisper, *I am here too.*
Feel that truth settle into your chest.
This is where leadership begins—not in control, but in
    recognition.

You do not disappear when you rest.
You return.
And in that return, your calm becomes real.

CHAPTER 2

The Weight of Strength

Language Cue: Resilient Fatigue
The gradual depletion that occurs when strength becomes a default response instead of a conscious choice.

The Echo After "I See You"

In the previous chapter, we looked at the toll of being unseen — the quiet ache of emotional masking, the way composure can turn into camouflage when you feel invisible in the spaces you're supposed to lead. But what happens when visibility comes back, and you still can't find rest? When the light finally spots you, yet your body stays tense, your voice remains measured, and your presence feels rehearsed?

There is a specific fatigue that appears when being seen still feels like performing. It's the exhaustion that lingers even after recognition, support, or acknowledgment arrives. This is the second layer of leadership tiredness — not invisibility, but overexposure. When your strength becomes something others depend on so constantly that you don't feel free to step outside of it. When being known still feels like being judged, and when the spotlight becomes another kind of burden.

Overexposure occurs when strength is worn out too long, too publicly, or too quietly. When your emotional endurance becomes part of people's expectations instead of your humanity. You are visible, yes — but only as the strong one, the steady one, the one who doesn't flinch. So the mask doesn't vanish; it becomes more subtle. Less camouflage, more costume.

This is the echo after "I see you."

The moment when seeing isn't enough, because what people see is the version of you you've crafted to survive. And while recognition can soothe invisibility, it cannot cure depletion. Visibility without authenticity becomes another stage where composure performs instead of restores.

This is where the next level of leadership fatigue shows itself — the gap between being seen and being supported, between being visible and being understood, between being strong and feeling safe enough to soften. It is in this gap that composure must develop, shifting from external expectations to internal integrity.

And that evolution starts with recognizing this truth: sometimes the hardest place to find rest is in plain sight.

Strength Has a Shelf Life

Strength is admirable — until it becomes rigid. At first, it feels noble to remain steady, to push forward, to bear the weight others can't. You take pride in being the anchor, the one who never wavers, the one others trust when everything else falls apart. But somewhere along the way, courage turns into currency — proof that you've earned your spot, your respect, your right to lead. And that's where the crack starts.

When strength becomes your identity rather than your intention, it becomes fragile. What once gave you purpose begins to drain it away. You wake up one morning and realize your strength no longer serves you — it's consuming you.

We seldom talk about the burden of strength because we are conditioned to admire its appearance, not its cost. We celebrate results — tenacity, endurance, achievement — but overlook the quiet toll underneath. Behind every confident professional stance is often someone who forgot to rest because the world rewarded their refusal to stop. That is resilient fatigue — the point when perseverance stops feeling like purpose and starts feeling like pressure.

The Performance of Power

Professional culture trains us to show strength long before it teaches us how to embody it. Early in your career, you observe leaders who never flinch, who power through meetings without pause, and who treat urgency as a virtue. You imitate their pace. You absorb their cadence. You internalize the myth that leadership is about constant action and controlled emotion.

Over time, you start to confuse emotional regulation with emotional suppression. You learn to control your tone while ignoring the truth. You speak with calm certainty even when your inner world feels cluttered or exhausted. Strength in performance appears to be control, but it is maintained through tension. It is composure built on contraction.

Eventually, you begin to mistake exhaustion for excellence, depletion for devotion, and speed for significance. The faster you go, the more vital you feel. The harder you push, the more worthy you think you appear. Rest starts to seem like weakness. Recovery becomes indulgence rather than discipline.

The body keeps moving forward out of habit, but the spirit quietly withdraws. Presence is replaced with performance. You operate with curated calm — steady on the surface, fragile underneath. That isn't leadership; it's survival theater. A practiced display of composure that masks the slow erosion of connection, creativity, and coherence.

The irony is devastating: the leader who appears unshakeable is often the one most at risk of collapse.

Real power relies on authenticity, not armor. It needs a nervous system that knows how to soften, a mind that can discern, and a heart free to feel. Without this inner harmony, power becomes a facade — impressive to others but harmful to yourself.

The Paradox of Resilience

Resilience is one of leadership's most celebrated and misunderstood virtues. We praise it in speeches, print it on posters, and assess it in performance reviews. Yet, resilience without reflection becomes repression. When endurance exceeds awareness, depletion becomes normal. The very behaviors that damage us are the ones we celebrate.

You begin to call your exhaustion "grit." You label sustained effort "dedication." You name ongoing overexertion "credibility."

This is how resilience turns into rigidity. What once protected you starts to trap you. You bend until you can't feel the bend anymore. You adapt until you don't recognize what you're adapting to.

True resilience isn't repetition — it's evolution. It's the ability to change form without losing your core. To stretch without breaking. To stay sensitive without becoming overwhelmed. Resilience isn't about suppressing emotion; it's about navigating it wisely.

This is adaptive capacity — the ability to restore balance rather than collapse into burnout. Adaptive capacity requires recognizing your needs, setting your limits, and pacing yourself. It is leadership that values humanity, not just productivity.

Within The Mosaic Way™, this is Identity Agility — the ability to adapt to change without losing your coherence. To stay true to yourself even as the environment shifts. Identity agility is a strength that bends rather than breaks, a presence that maintains both endurance and empathy simultaneously.

When resilience evolves into agility, composure becomes more than just survival — it turns into stability. You don't merely endure pressure; you reshape it. And those around you sense not your tension but your steadiness, not your performance but your presence.

That is the paradox: leadership grows stronger when you stop showcasing strength and start living in coherence.

When Courage Turns into Containment

Leaders who carry too much for too long often mistake endurance for empathy. What starts as strength gradually becomes a silent standard everyone around you tries to meet. You think, "If I can handle this, they can too." Unknowingly, you start judging others by your capacity rather than their reality. You view their needs through the filter of your own limits. Over time, this kind of courage shifts into containment — a quiet constriction that narrows the emotional space around you.

Containment doesn't appear suddenly; it shows up quietly. You start holding everything together so tightly that those around you begin holding their breath. They approach cautiously. They hold back. They hesitate to disturb your rhythm because your stability feels sacred but unreachable. You hear phrases like, "You've already got so much going on," or "I didn't want to add to your load." On the surface, these sound like respect. In reality, they indicate relational distancing.

This distance isn't caused by fear of your anger — it's caused by fear of your exhaustion. People don't want to break what seems unbreakable. They avoid sharing concerns, emotions, or mistakes because your composure feels too perfect to disturb. What was once courage becomes a barrier others don't feel safe to open.

Composure without accessibility becomes detachment. And courage without compassion slowly shifts into control — not the loud, domineering kind, but the quiet pressure that influences how others behave around you. When people think they need to "protect" you from more stress, you lose honest feedback, open dialogue, and shared emotional effort that healthy leadership depends on.

The paradox is this: the more tightly you hold things, the less people feel held by you.

True composure creates space, not restriction. It signals: You can bring your full self here. It's not your unbreakability that draws people closer; it's your humanity. When courage is combined with compassion, it becomes connection. When strength is paired with softness, it becomes safety.

Leadership thrives not when you contain everything, but when you create the conditions where no one has to hold their breath — including you.

The Body Keeps Score of Control

Leadership is often taught as a cognitive act — think clearly, speak strategically, decide decisively. But the body is always the first to notice what the mind tries to ignore. Emotional weight never truly leaves; it just shifts. It settles in your shoulders, tightening with every expectation you agree to bear alone. It locks into your jaw, clenching around words you weren't ready to say. It appears as the 3 a.m. wake-up that won't let you go, even when you're exhausted. It lingers in the shallow breath between back-to-back meetings and the quiet scrolling before bed because stillness feels more threatening than noise.

This is the body keeping score — not of failure, but of control. Every time you push past your limits, your nervous system records it. Every time you suppress an emotion in the name of professionalism, your body absorbs the toll. Over time, what appears to be composure on the surface becomes tension beneath. The body turns into a storage space for unspoken truths, a living record of every moment you told yourself you could go a little further.

But your nervous system isn't betraying you; it's informing you. It is the most honest leader you have. Tightness, fatigue, irritability, restlessness—these are not weaknesses to hide; they are signals of intelligence. They are data. They are early warnings that something in your leadership rhythm is out of sync.

Embodied integrity begins the moment you stop dismissing those signals. Composure is not the absence of sensation; it is the ability to interpret it. When your body whispers, *slow down*; that is composure calling you back into coherence. When it signals, *not this pace, not this load*, it is offering you guidance wiser than any strategic plan.

The language of leadership is not just spoken; it also involves physical presence. Tone is felt before it is heard, and presence is sensed before it is fully understood. When you begin to honor your body as a source of intelligence — rather than an obstacle to be bypassed — you move beyond merely acting resilient and start truly living resiliently. You shift from simply performing strength to embodying it.

In The Mosaic Way™, this is where emotional integrity deepens into embodiment: when your inner truth aligns with your outer presence, and your leadership becomes not just a performance to uphold, but a rhythm you can maintain.

The Myth of Limitless Capacity

Every organization has its own mythology. One of the most alluring — and risky — is the myth of unlimited capacity: the belief that great leaders can do more with less forever, that resilience is measured by volume, and that worth is proven through exhaustion. We praise the relentless worker, reward the earliest riser, and admire the leader who never seems to break. In doing so, we confuse systemic fatigue with dedication and overextension with excellence.

But capacity without limits is not leadership; it's leakage. When everything flows out, and nothing flows back in, clarity vanishes first, then creativity, and finally compassion. The leader remains active but no longer attuned. Decisions become efficient but not wise. Presence remains consistent, but no longer connects. This is the hidden tax of limitless performance — a cost paid in pieces of yourself.

Each unexamined "yes" drains the energy needed for reflection, innovation, and relational steadiness. Overcommitment is not loyalty; it's self-abandonment disguised as service. It signals a culture that has mistaken endurance for devotion and busyness for belonging. When leaders normalize depletion, teams learn to mirror it. The myth spreads — not through words, but through the atmosphere.

Strong leaders don't just maximize capacity; they curate it. They realize that energy is an ecosystem, not a bank account. It needs to be nourished, protected, and periodically renewed. They understand that sustainable excellence requires a rhythm — seasons of intensity balanced with intentional recovery. When energy is regarded as a renewable resource rather than an endless one, leadership becomes healthier, more strategic, and more humane.

Sustainability isn't self-indulgence; it's ethical leadership. A depleted leader can't foster psychological safety. A scattered leader can't promote clarity. A leader who has forsaken their own humanity can't guide others. By protecting your capacity, you strengthen the group. You model a leadership style that doesn't exploit itself or others — the foundation of true collective care.

The myth of unlimited capacity falls apart the moment a leader prioritizes coherence over exhaustion. When you respect your limits, you encourage your team to respect theirs. You foster a culture where excellence is maintained, not drained — where people are recognized not for how much they can endure, but for how intentionally they deploy their strength.

Mosaic in Action: The Leader Who Finally Exhaled

During a regional strategy offsite, a director sat at the edge of a conference table surrounded by charts, timelines, and ambitious goals. When the facilitator asked how everyone was truly doing — not professionally, but personally — she hesitated. Then she admitted something she had never said aloud: she hadn't taken a single weekend off in months. "If I rest," she murmured, "people think I've lost my edge. I'm afraid slowing down will look like slipping."

The room grew silent. When asked to pick one word that described her current state, she gazed at the carpet for a moment before whispering, "Tense." The word carried a weight that even surprised her. It wasn't burnout she feared — it was being seen as anything less than unbreakable.

Over the next quarter, she tried something surprisingly simple: she added a fifteen-minute pause to her calendar each afternoon. Not a task, not a meeting—just a protected break of time with no obligations. She stepped outside. She sat by a window. She took a deep breath. Some days she journaled; other days she did nothing at all. It wasn't the length of the pause that mattered — it was the permission.

Within weeks, the change was clear. Her decision-making improved because she no longer approached choices with a clenched attitude. Her tone softened, not from weakness, but from clarity. Her team noticed the difference first. They stopped rushing to match her intensity and started matching her steadiness. Meetings became calmer. Conflicts are resolved more quickly. The department's pace became sustainable again — because she stopped showing urgency as a sign of excellence.

This is the paradox of strength: the moment you stop trying to prove it, is the moment you start to live it. Rest did not lessen her leadership; it strengthened it. Her presence became steadier, her communication more in tune, her influence more relatable.

In The Mosaic Way™, this practice is called Restorative Modeling—the art of guiding others into balance by exemplifying it yourself. It recognizes that the nervous system of an entire team often follows its leader's rhythm. When she finally exhaled, her department realized they could do the same.

The Mosaic Advantage Reframed

Within The Mosaic Way™, composure is not just a behavior — it is the convergence of three interconnected abilities that influence how you lead under pressure and how others perceive you in that pressure. These capacities work together like interconnected pieces of a living framework, each one strengthening the stability of the others.

Emotional integrity is the internal harmony between your feelings, values, and the leadership you provide. When you deny your exhaustion or ignore signs of strain, you break that harmony. You start performing steadiness instead of truly living it. Emotional integrity invites honesty: *How am I, really? And is the way I'm leading in line with what I say I care about?* Without this alignment, composure becomes a mask rather than a genuine practice.

Cultural Flexibility recognizes that expressions of strength are not universal. What appears confident in one culture may seem dismissive in another; what feels direct in one context may seem disrespectful in another. Flexibility isn't watering down the truth — it's expanding perspective. It's the ability to stay true to yourself while accommodating others' ways of communicating, processing, and contributing.

Flexible leaders foster trust because they show that connection matters as much as clarity.

Identity Agility grants you permission to evolve without losing your core self. It marks the shift from believing you must handle everything alone to recognizing you can share the workload without sacrificing competence or credibility. Agility broadens your sense of belonging. It enables you to adapt, pivot, and expand your leadership identity while staying grounded in who you are becoming.

When these three capacities move together, strength ceases to be rigid. It becomes rhythmic — steady without stiffness, grounded without defensiveness. You stop clutching and start anchoring. You stop holding your breath and begin inhabiting your presence. This is the core of grounded awareness: stability not from control, but from coherence. It is leadership that breathes, adapts, and resonates.

Leadership Fatigue as a Silent Epidemic

Across industries, studies confirm the rise of leadership exhaustion—a silent epidemic masked by calmness. Ask any senior leader how they're doing, and the usual response is: *I'm fine*.

"I'm fine" has become the corporate code for suppressing emotions. Behind it lie insomnia, decision fatigue, relational drift, and the ache of unacknowledged isolation.

This isn't incompetence; it's culture — a culture that links visibility with vulnerability and productivity with worth. We have normalized the harmful cycle of overperformance and called it ambition. But ambition without attunement leads directly to collapse.

The world doesn't need leaders who can carry more; it needs leaders who can feel more — responsibly, courageously, and humanly.

Studies from the American Psychological Association and McKinsey's *Women in the Workplace* report confirm that burnout has become leadership's most costly hidden expense. Nearly 60 percent of senior leaders report chronic exhaustion, and one in three consider stepping back or resigning due to mental health concerns. The pattern is clear: when resilience is used as endurance, attrition becomes the body's rebellion.

From Holding to Honoring

Imagine strength not as weight you carry but as energy you manage. That simple shift — from holding to honoring — transforms everything. When you honor your strength, you see it as dynamic, responsive, and alive. You understand that it expands and contracts with seasons, circumstances, and self-awareness.

You stop measuring your worth by endurance and begin measuring it by recovery literacy — the wisdom to know when to pause, not just when to push. Honoring strength means trading balance for rhythm. Some seasons demand intensity; others invite restoration. Composure discerns the difference. Strength no longer needs to prove itself. It simply needs permission to breathe.

In emotionally intelligent systems, recovery is not a retreat from performance — it is part of performance. The most sustainable leaders intentionally and repeatedly incorporate rhythms of rest into their workflows, as they do with strategy. Recovery literacy asks, *How do I rebuild energy as actively as I use it?*

When rest stops being merely a reward and turns into a routine, composure shifts from reactionary to relational — something that stabilizes not only you but everyone around you.

Micro-Moment Practice: The 30-Second Reset

When you feel yourself tightening under pressure, pause. Drop your shoulders and unclench your jaw. Breathe in through your nose for four counts, hold for two, and exhale slowly for six. Silently tell yourself, "This is weight, not weakness." Then ask, *"What requires attention — me, them, or the moment?"*

This thirty-second ritual reprograms the nervous system for psychological flexibility. Over time, it becomes a habitual state of calm. Leaders who practice it regularly report less reactivity, deeper listening, and more empathy under pressure.

Composure isn't formed through large gestures; it's developed through small moments of awareness that help the body relearn what safety feels like.

Rewriting the Narrative of Strength

You do not owe the world your exhaustion. You owe it your example. Leadership was never meant to be proven by depletion. Yet many high-capacity leaders have been conditioned to believe that strength is measured by strain — by how much you can endure, carry, solve, or silence. But exhaustion is not evidence of excellence; it indicates imbalance.

Strength is not what you sacrifice; it's what you maintain. It is not your willingness to absorb more pressure, but your ability to process it with clarity. Strength is not measured by how long you can go without rest, but by how purposefully you return to rest. In this new perspective, recovery becomes part of responsibility, and pacing becomes part of professionalism.

When you redefine strength as stewardship rather than strain, a new culture takes shape—a culture where resilience and rest coexist rather than compete. Where ambition is driven by awareness, not adrenaline, where capacity grows not through overextension, but through coherence, this shift breaks down the myth that leadership requires self-erasure. Instead, it recognizes that your presence — not your performance — is the most stabilizing force you offer.

In such a culture, leaders stop showcasing burnout as a badge of honor. They start demonstrating balance as a sign of integrity. They realize that sustainability is not a weakness; it is a strategy. Rest becomes an essential part of preparation. Reflection becomes a key part of productivity. Emotional clarity becomes vital for effective execution.

This exemplifies The Mosaic Advantage™: emotional fluency that not only grounds the leader but also sustains the systems they support. It is leadership that heals rather than harms, expands rather than exhausts, and influences through coherence rather than control. It is strength redefined — steady, conscious, regenerative.

The future of leadership won't depend on how much you can push yourself, but on how well you stay aligned while guiding others. That alignment isn't just about personal wellness; it's about organizational wisdom. It starts the moment you change your relationship with strength — shifting from survival to stewardship, from depletion to design, from pressure to presence.

Reflection —
The Question Beneath the Calm

Before you turn the page, take a moment for an honest check-in. Ask yourself:

- When has strength become performance rather than practice?
- Which emotions have I mistaken for productivity?
- How might my leadership change if I saw recovery as a responsibility instead of a reward?

You don't need to abandon your strength. You need to let it breathe.

Because true composure isn't about carrying everything — it's about understanding what's worth carrying, and why.

In the next chapter, we'll explore what that breath becomes— how emotional fluency turns stillness into strength, and composure into connection.

!

The Data That Demands Attention

The myth of endless resilience still comes with a real cost. A 2024 Gallup global study found that 44 percent of workers experience "daily stress" at work, the highest rate since tracking began. The U.S. Surgeon General has called workplace burnout a public health crisis, linking it to anxiety, absenteeism, and lower productivity.

For leaders, the data becomes even more revealing. In Deloitte's 2023 "Women at Work" report, nearly half of women in leadership roles said they felt "exhausted" or "on the verge of burnout." Among men, recent McKinsey data showed that one in three senior leaders is actively considering stepping down to protect their mental health. The culture of overextension—once seen as a sign of commitment—has now become a liability.

When strength is measured solely by endurance, it results in emotional depletion disguised as dedication. The evidence is clear: those who learn to balance effort with recovery perform better than those who don't. Resilience must grow from mere survival into a process of renewal.

A Word to the Generations

Generation X

You were taught that strength meant being stoic. But even iron rusts without proper care. Let your steadiness be sustainable by acknowledging what costs too much.

Millennials

You've carried the language of resilience through recessions, layoffs, and uncertainty. You no longer need to prove your endurance. Your strength now lies in protecting your energy.

Generation Z

You instinctively reject burnout culture—and that instinct is wise. Redefine success as alignment, not overextension. You can pause without losing purpose.

Generation Alpha

The world will expect consistent effort from you. Remember that recovery is not retreat. Learn early that rest is strength in motion.

Generation Beta

You will inherit systems that reward endurance. Learn early that strength is not proving you can hold everything—but choosing what is not yours to carry.

Which part of your generational voice feels strongest right now—clarity, connection, speed, or listening?

The Composed Practice

Composed — Chapter 2: The Weight of Strength

Resilience · Release · Permission to Rest

Strength is not about what I lift; it's about what I let go of.
I can be powerful without being cold or unfeeling.
I'm allowed to rest.

Breathe deeply.
Notice where your body tightens when you think about
holding everything together.
That tension is the cost of carrying what was never meant to
be permanent.

You have worn endurance like armor, mistaking strain for
importance. But strength is not endless endurance; it is
wisdom. It is knowing when to stand your ground and
when to show compassion.

Place one hand on your chest and softly say, *I am strong
enough to be human.*
Let that phrase resonate in the silence. Resting is not a
weakness; it is a form of wisdom that reconnects you
with yourself.

Even the strongest structures need to pause between storms.
So do you.

CHAPTER 3 ———————————————

What Composure Really Means

Language Cue: Emotional Fluency

The capacity to recognize, interpret, and integrate emotion in real time — not as a disruption to leadership, but as its deepest form of intelligence.

The Bridge From Strength to Stillness

In the previous chapter, we examined the nature of strength — how carrying so much for so long can turn endurance into wear. Strength helps you carry on, but strength alone doesn't keep everything connected. It supports, it pushes, it persists — but without something to soften the edges, strength becomes a quiet burden.

What sustains leaders is not force but fluency — the ability to move with emotion rather than against it. Fluency is the internal agility that allows you to interpret what you feel instead of absorbing it, redirect intensity instead of reacting to it, and stay present without being overwhelmed. If strength is the body of composure, fluency is its breath. It transforms effort into rhythm, pressure into clarity, and survival into stability.

Fluency serves as the link between action and being. It enables a strong leader to also become calm — someone who reacts less, observes more, and remains composed amid chaos without disconnecting. Strength might carry you through the storm, but fluency helps you find meaning within it. It is the space between stimulus and response, the quiet internal voice that keeps your leadership human.

This is where true composure deepens: not when you hold everything together through force, but when you learn to navigate your emotions with fidelity, curiosity, and ease. Strength supports you, but fluency frees you. Together, they make stillness possible.

The Quiet in the Chaos

Composure is not about being completely still; it's about maintaining awareness. The world hardly ever slows down for anyone. Deadlines tighten, expectations increase, and uncertainty becomes the new normal. Amid that constant movement, a leader's role isn't to micromanage the chaos but to stay connected to themselves within it.

For years, we have seen composure as endurance — standing firm while everything around us shakes. But endurance is only the surface. Beneath it lies a connection. True composure is not avoiding emotion but being in harmony with it — emotional clarity and grounded awareness intertwined. It is the quiet acceptance that chaos outside cannot erase the order within.

Calm, then, isn't the beginning of composure — it's the reflection. It shows up when your thoughts, values, and emotions are in sync. You stop acting peaceful and start being it; you stop pretending to lead with strength and start leading through presence.

The Architecture of Awareness

Composure depends on three key elements: awareness, alignment, and acceptance. Awareness identifies what's happening inside you before it shows as behavior. Alignment transforms that awareness into actions that reflect emotional honesty rather than insecurity. Acceptance permits imperfection and purpose to coexist without judgment.

When these three elements align, you operate from your core instead of your edges; you respond instead of react. This is an architecture of awareness — internal stability that pressure cannot steal.

Many leaders realize awareness only after something breaks: a harsh word spoken in frustration, a restless night, or crossing a value in the pursuit of speed. Composure allows for earlier recognition — the tremor before the crack. With consistent practice, awareness becomes emotional fluency in motion: you interpret your own cues as clearly as your calendar.

The Myth of Detachment

Modern leadership often advocates detachment as the opposite of composure. They are not the same. Detachment is about creating distance; composure is about maintaining depth. To detach means to disconnect — to appear unbothered, unshaken, unreachable. It might feel safe temporarily, but it leaves the leader hollow inside.

Detachment isolates; composure unites. A detached leader says, don't feel. A composed leader says, feel fully — just don't let the feeling control you. That distinction changes everything. It allows empathy without becoming overly involved and accountability without being aggressive.

It transforms emotion from a distraction into insight. True composure isn't about remaining unaffected; it's about staying in tune. You can experience the feeling and stay steady, fostering trust instead of hiding behind authority.

The Space Between Reaction and Response

Between each trigger and decision, there's a pause—a sacred fraction of a second where instinct halts, and intention begins. That pause is where composure is formed.

Reaction is instinct; response is intelligence. Composed leaders refuse to rush the moment. They breathe, observe, and listen to the pulse of the situation before acting. That small pause lowers a room's emotional temperature, restores clarity in conflict, and prevents one person's stress from spiraling into everyone's.

In that practice, you become a thermostat instead of a thermometer — setting the tone rather than absorbing it — and your psychological flexibility helps stabilize the group.

Mosaic in Action: The Leader Who Paused Before Speaking

During a tense budget review, a department head listened as a colleague questioned the accuracy of her team's data. She felt the familiar heat rise — the tightness in her chest, her thoughts quickening, and a natural surge of defensiveness. She knew exactly how this moment usually played out: point-by-point rebuttals, stiff tones, and a meeting sidetracked by ego rather than insight. The room seemed to brace for impact.

But this time, she chose something different. She put down her pen, closed her eyes briefly, and let her nervous system calm down. When she opened them again, her tone had softened. Her presence shifted from reactive to receptive.

"Before I respond," she said calmly, "I want to understand what feels unclear."

The atmosphere shifted instantly. The rising tension eased. Her colleague leaned in instead of pulling back. The critique turned into curiosity. What could have led to conflict instead became cooperation. The budget discussion changed from a defensive argument into a productive conversation about assumptions, data sources, and shared goals.

Her team later said they noticed the change in real time — not only in the meeting's outcome but also in the emotional tone she established. That single breath prevented the room from breaking apart. It turned a possible rupture into an opportunity for clarity. It reminded everyone there that leadership isn't about quick answers but about steady presence.

In that moment, emotional fluency stopped being just a concept on a page and became a real experience. She wasn't suppressing her frustration; she was managing it. She wasn't pretending to be composed; she was embodying it. Her pause made enough space for truth to replace tension and for understanding to replace defensiveness.

That is The Mosaic Way™ in action — self-awareness shaping tone, tone shaping connection, and connection shaping the outcome.

The Mirror of Emotion

Every emotion shows what you value. Anger signals a boundary has been broken. Fear uncovers where trust has failed. Sadness reveals where attachment still exists.

Once you understand this, you stop viewing emotion as weakness and start seeing it as wisdom. Emotions are not distractions; they are data — vital inputs for aligning your values and making better decisions.

Yet many leaders were taught to focus on appearances instead of authentic energy, suppressing emotions in the name of "professionalism." Neutrality was rewarded even when it lacked sincerity.

Composure promotes honesty without breaking down. It encourages you to listen before judging and to become fluent in your inner voice so that emotion educates you, rather than rules dominate you.

When Calm Becomes Courage

Calm isn't about adherence; it's about bravery — the bravery to slow down when everything around you speeds up. It requires courage to pause instead of react, to breathe instead of brace, to stay open when others shut down. Courage isn't always loud. Sometimes, it's the quiet choice to interrupt your own instinct for self-protection long enough to stay human.

True composure requires the strength to admit uncertainty in a world that rewards premature confidence. It asks you to choose reflection over performance, clarity over speed, and presence over posturing. These decisions are not signs of hesitation; they are acts of leadership. They declare that urgency will not control your values, and pressure will not determine your tone.

Composure becomes a moral act when you refuse to let chaos alter your character. When you choose not to reflect the aggression, panic, or defensiveness around you. When you defend your sense of belonging — your place within yourself — more fiercely than you defend your ego. In this way, calm becomes a quiet form of resistance against environments that mistake haste for strength and volume for conviction.

In its purest form, calmness is not the absence of energy but the mastery of it. It is the shift from control to coherence — from forcing outcomes to guiding intention, from managing impressions to embodying integrity. True composure becomes courage when your steadiness isn't performative, but grounded in principles. When your calm is not a mask but a message: I will not abandon who I am, even here.

This kind of calm doesn't silence emotion; it channels it. It transforms noise into clarity, pressure into focus, presence into influence. Leaders who practice this form of courage don't just stabilize the room — they elevate it.

The Discipline of Return

Even the most emotionally skilled leaders lose their center. We all do. Composure was never meant to be a posture of perfection — it is a practice of return. The real question isn't whether you will tilt, tighten, or momentarily lose alignment. It's how quickly, consciously, and kindly you find your way back.

Return requires humility. It asks you to recognize when your tone hardens, your patience wears thin, or your presence turns into performance. It encourages you to resist the urge to justify or defend and instead choose to repair. This kind of repair isn't a sign of weakness; it's a sign of maturity. It shows that you value relationship more than ego, clarity more than pride, and growth more than image.

When you return without shame, you teach others that composure is based on honesty, not on perfect performance. You demonstrate that leadership isn't measured by how rarely you stumble but by how reliably you readjust. The return follows a rhythm — a straight-forward, steady pattern that becomes second nature over time.

Recognize: Notice the moment you've drifted.
Identify: Name the feeling, the trigger, or the misalignment.
Re-align: Choose the next action that brings you back into coherence.

This is not a dramatic transformation; it is a disciplined recalibration. Small resets. Quiet adjustments. Subtle shifts in breath, language, posture, or pace.

That is the Mosaic rhythm — systemic resilience built through intentional micro-repairs rather than performative displays of control. It's the kind of composure that becomes contagious, helping teams recover faster, communicate more honestly, and navigate tension with less fear. Leaders who master the discipline of return cultivate environments where missteps are met with reflection instead of punishment and where humanity is not a liability but a source of strength.

In this rhythm, returning isn't a retreat; it's a restoration. It brings you back to yourself — and encourages others to follow suit.

The Language of Alignment

Words form the basis of composure; they are not neutral. Every phrase carries energy — either restoring balance or causing disruption. A leader who asks, "What's happening for you?" opens a doorway to honesty. A leader who asks, "What's wrong with you?" builds a wall of shame. Tone decides whether people step forward or start to shrink.

Language is one of the most precise tools in emotionally intelligent leadership.

"Take your time" communicates partnership;
"Calm down" communicates judgment.
The first relaxes the nervous system.
The second activates defense.

This is because language is more than just expression — it is about regulation. Your words can lower or raise cortisol levels. They can make a space feel larger or smaller. They can foster belonging or cause division. Leaders often underestimate how much emotional interpretation takes place in the gaps between their sentences.

Emotionally fluent leaders speak not to impress but to connect. Their words focus on clarity, compassion, and coherence. They understand that words don't just reflect reality — they shape it. A phrase delivered with intention can restore psychological safety; one spoken without care can break it down.

That's why having a shared vocabulary is important. A team without a common language ends up guessing, interpreting, or assuming — often wrongly. But when teams share clear definitions for concepts like tension, overwhelm, clarity, or repair, emotional misunderstandings decrease, and collaboration gets better. A shared glossary becomes a common foundation. It turns into the emotional infrastructure that helps people express needs, negotiate pace, and work together without fear or confusion.

When leaders select words that reflect their integrity, their language becomes a stabilizing force. It aligns people not just with expectations but also with each other.

Control Versus Composure

Control and composure are often mistaken for each other, but they come from completely different places. Control is fear hiding behind a mask of authority — the idea that if you manage everything, nothing will fall apart. It's based on hypervigilance, not wisdom. It can keep a system running, but it can't keep a system truly connected.

Composure, on the other hand, is trust made real. It is the embodied confidence that *even if everything shifts, I can remain whole.* Composure doesn't tighten; it steadies. It doesn't demand compliance; it cultivates clarity. Leaders driven by control hold their breath. Leaders rooted in composure help everyone else exhale.

Control promotes isolation. It creates a situation where people turn to you for answers but hide their questions. It values perfection over connection and conformity over creativity. In contrast, composure encourages connection — the feeling that everyone can contribute honestly without fear of punishment. Composure isn't about dominance; it's about harmony, the alignment of energy that allows teams to work with both speed and purpose.

In uncertain times, composure becomes a new kind of leadership currency. People no longer trust certainty — too much in the world shifts too quickly for that. Instead, they trust steadiness. They follow leaders whose presence feels like oxygen in rooms that have forgotten how to breathe. They follow the one who listens without assuming, pauses without retreating, and speaks with clarity instead of pressure.

Control constricts, but composure expands. Control maintains the system; composure sustains the people within it. And when people feel safe, the system thrives.

This is the core of The Mosaic Way™ — leadership not just as performance but as coherence. Leaders who embody this shift do more than guide teams; they restore the emotional environment where teams can thrive.

Stillness as Intelligence

Stillness is not passivity; it is perception. When you pause, your nervous system shifts from survival mode to synthesis. Patterns emerge that speed hides. Research from Harvard's Center for Emotional Intelligence and Stanford's Mind, Brain, and Behavior Lab shows that brief pauses—just three conscious breaths—shift neural activity from the amygdala (reactivity) to the prefrontal cortex (reason). In that moment, leaders regain access to empathy, problem-solving, and perspective.

This is the neuroscience of composure: when the nervous system relaxes, wisdom emerges again. Stillness reorganizes the mosaic inside you. It gathers scattered pieces — responsibility, identity, fatigue — and restores coherence. In stillness, you remember the self beneath performance and regain a sense of safety in your identity, allowing you to act from truth rather than perceived threat.

The Moral Dimension of Composure

At its highest level, composure is not just a skill — it is an ethical position. It is the quiet discipline of choosing truth without cruelty, clarity without control, and steadiness without emotional withdrawal. Composure becomes moral when it safeguards the humanity of others while respecting the integrity of your own. It is what enables leaders to speak difficult truths with kindness, to set boundaries without humiliation, and to provide presence in systems that value urgency more than understanding.

In this context, tone becomes a form of justice. The way you speak — your pace, your volume, your choice of words — signals whether people are safe, respected, and allowed to be fully human in your presence. Tone can either elevate or diminish. It can protect the fragile space where ideas form, and identities collide, or it can collapse that space altogether. When used intentionally, tone becomes leadership's most accessible tool for fairness: guidance without control, direction without intimidation, and influence without erasure.

Composure is therefore not passive. It is an active moral commitment to consistency, care, and accountability. Your steadiness demonstrates a truth often forgotten in high-pressure environments: that dignity and responsibility do not compete. They coexist. They shape each other. They enable the work to continue without sacrificing people's sense of worth.

Ethical composure is the refusal to weaponize authority. It is the courage to stay present when conversations become uncomfortable, and the humility to manage your emotions so you don't take unprocessed feelings out on others. It is leadership without causing harm — not by avoiding conflict, but by handling it with respect.

When leaders embody this moral dimension, calm is more than an emotional state; it becomes a cultural signal. It communicates: We can tell the truth here. We can disagree here. We can repair here. *We can be human here.*

This is composure as justice — not softness, but integrity in action.

The Mosaic of Self-Regulation

Inside each of us, a mosaic of selves exists — the performer who strives to succeed, the protector who wants to keep us safe, the learner who seeks new possibilities, the doubter who prepares for disappointment. Each part is shaped by memory, culture, identity, and experience. Under pressure, these selves don't vanish; they compete for the microphone, rushing to the front of the stage, each convinced it knows how to best protect us.

Composure isn't about silencing these voices — it's about mediating between them. It involves internal leadership that ensures every part of you feels acknowledged without allowing any one part to dominate. Self-regulation doesn't mean silencing the alarmed, impatient, or anxious parts; it means recognizing their signals, giving them healthier roles, and restoring internal harmony.

When the performer softens, presence is free to guide.

When the protector relaxes, curiosity can return to the room.

When the doubter is reassured, discernment comes back instead of fear.

When the learner speaks, innovation becomes possible.

This is how inner coherence develops: not by force, but through your relationship with yourself.

And the more consistent your internal leadership becomes, the more credible your external leadership appears. People trust leaders whose tone aligns with their truth — whose composure is genuine, not performative, and whose steadiness comes from deliberate practice, not a mask.

Within **The Mosaic Way**™, composure symbolizes the equilibrium among all three capacities:

Emotional Integrity keeps you calm, honest, and grounded in truth rather than suppression.

Cultural Flexibility keeps you calm, inclusive, and aware of the impact your tone has across identities and contexts.

Identity Agility keeps you calm and authentic, allowing you to shift and adapt without abandoning yourself.

When these capacities move in harmony, calmness ceases to function as a set of behaviors and becomes something deeper: resonance. It is no longer the management of emotion but the alignment of energy. You stop controlling your internal world and begin directing it — with clarity, compassion, and precision.

This is leadership as coherence in action: the ability to gather your many selves, honor their wisdom, and still speak with one voice. The voice that reflects who you truly are.

Composure as Connection

The truest proof of composure isn't silence — it's connection. Anyone can seem calm when alone; stillness is simple when nothing's at stake. But true composure shows its real strength when relationships come into play. A composed leader doesn't just stay quiet; they stay engaged. They remain steady when tension rises, curious during disagreement, and calm when feelings run high. Their calm isn't withdrawal — it's engagement without becoming overwhelmed.

Composure combines intensity with presence. It does not dismiss emotion or see it as something to "manage" away. Instead, it views emotion as a bridge — a way to understand what someone is trying to protect, express, or hold together. This perspective turns conflict from a threat into an opportunity. It helps difficult conversations become spaces of clarity instead of moments of collapse.

In this way, composure becomes a form of leadership influence rooted not in authority but in resonance. You guide the room through example rather than command. Your steadiness becomes contagious. People regulate themselves through your presence because you show that it is possible to stay grounded without becoming rigid, honest without becoming harsh, and accountable without becoming punitive.

This exemplifies cultural attunement—responding to emotion and identity with respect, nuance, and awareness. When your composure shows both dignity and accountability, people feel safer sharing truth, offering perspective, and engaging in repair. They realize they don't have to sacrifice their humanity to be heard.

Trust, then, is not demanded. It is cultivated. It develops naturally around leaders whose calm does not silence others, but makes room for them.

Composure as connection is when emotional awareness deepens into relational wisdom — where how you hold yourself influences how you hold the room.

Reflection — Returning to the Center

Pause for an honest check-in:

- What emotion am I managing instead of mastering?
- Where am I confusing control with composure?
- How might stillness be a strategic strength in my week ahead?

Composure isn't the end of feeling; it's the start of understanding. When you can identify what moves you, you no longer fear change. You become the calm within the current — not because the current stops, but because you know who you are inside it.

In the next chapter, we turn inward again — into the realm of Emotional Integrity, where alignment replaces performance and coherence becomes the true measure of strength.

!

The Data That Demands Attention

Emotional fluency—not suppression—now characterizes effective leadership. In a 2024 Harvard Business Review study, 67 percent of employees reported performing better for managers who exhibit emotional clarity rather than emotional control. Leaders who accurately identify emotions build trust 31 percent higher and achieve notably stronger collaboration outcomes.

Conversely, the cost of emotional silence can be quantified. According to Korn Ferry's 2023 "Leadership in Transition" report, 58 percent of senior leaders admit they hide their emotions in critical moments out of fear of appearing unprofessional. However, organizations where leaders demonstrate authentic composure—calmness rooted in awareness, not avoidance—experience a 40 percent decrease in turnover intentions and greater team adaptability during crises.

The data confirms what experience already suggests: composure is not the absence of feeling but the regulation of it. The future of leadership will belong to those who can stay emotionally present without becoming emotionally reactive.

A Word to the Generations

Generation X — You mastered composure through control, but now the world values presence. Let your steadiness include emotional honesty — it strengthens, not weakens, your credibility.

Millennials — You grew up transforming emotion into empathy at work. Keep that gift, but protect it with discernment. Composure is not just performance; it's awareness paired with boundaries.

Generation Z — You embrace emotional language that others once avoided. Use it wisely. Ground your authenticity in skill, not impulse, and your influence will grow.

Generation Alpha — You will inherit leaders who speak openly about feelings. Learn early to combine that openness with self-control. Calm is not silence—it's clarity in action.

Generation Beta — You will be surrounded by instant response. Composure will not mean speed, but discernment—knowing when to pause before you participate.

Which part of your generational voice feels strongest right now—clarity, connection, speed, or listening?

The Composed Practice

Composed — Chapter 3:
What Composure Really Means

Awareness · Alignment · Emotional Fluency

I do not silence emotion; I interpret it. Calm isn't the absence
of feeling—it's the presence of understanding.
I can stand in the storm and stay whole.

Pause before moving on to the next part of your day.
Listen to your breath, the quiet rhythm that never demands
but always restores.
In this pause, you are not avoiding the world—you are
realigning with it.

You have spent years equating calm with control.
But control contracts; awareness expands.
Composure exists not in your jawline or your posture, but in
the space between reaction and response.

Whisper softly to yourself, I am safe to feel.
Let that truth loosen what effort has kept too tight. You are
not fragile for needing peace; you are fluent enough to
return to it.

Stillness is not your refuge. It is your intelligence in action.

PART II —————————————————

The Mosaic Within

Language Cue: Inner Alignment
The process of returning to your center—where values, emotions, and identity begin to move in the same rhythm again.

The Battle Within

There comes a moment in every leader's life when you realize that the loudest battles aren't the ones happening around you—they're the ones quietly fought within you.

You've mastered the art of staying calm amid chaos. You've learned to lead teams, resolve crises, and carry the invisible weight of responsibility without breaking. But somewhere between the meetings and milestones, you start to lose your sense of self.

That's the quiet truth most leadership frameworks never face: success can pull you out of alignment just as easily as failure can.

The more responsibility you bear, the more likely you are to fragment—to split yourself into different parts for each situation you encounter. One version for the workplace. Another for the boardroom. Yet another for the people you love. And deep beneath all that adaptation lies the real you—the one who remembers why you started leading in the first place.

53

Part II of this book focuses on rediscovering that version. It's about reclaiming your internal coherence—the Mosaic within you that leadership was never meant to erase.

The Hidden Fragmentation

Every leader starts with purpose—a spark of belief that leadership can create significance. But over time, systems, politics, and constant expectations teach us to adapt—often at the cost of authenticity. You learn which emotions are "acceptable." You learn how to speak without giving away too much. You learn that honesty must be managed, not openly shared.

That is how fragmentation begins. It's rarely sudden; it's gradual. You start defending your role at the expense of your wholeness. You trade authenticity for conformity.

The Mosaic Within encourages you to flip that perspective. It urges you to view composure not as a performance but as an ongoing practice—the skill of staying internally balanced even as the world changes around you. Composure that lacks emotional authenticity, cultural adaptability, and identity fluidity is just a facade; under pressure, it crumbles.

The upcoming chapters aren't about adding new leadership tactics. They're about shedding what no longer serves you—the layers of pretense, fear, and conditioning that block your true self. When those layers fall away, what's left isn't emptiness. It's essence. It's the part of you that never needed fixing—only permission.

Wholeness as Strategy

In modern leadership, we've made a dangerous mistake: treating wholeness as a wellness goal instead of a strategic necessity. We push it aside for offsites, retreats, and self-care weekends. But wholeness isn't something you achieve after the work is done—it's what makes the work sustainable from the start.

When you lead from alignment, your decisions become easier, your relationships feel more genuine, and your presence appears more natural. You stop wasting emotional energy trying to show strength. You start leading with clarity instead of choreography.

That's the promise of *The Mosaic Advantage*™: the ability to lead from your core without being torn apart by competing demands. It's not about balance—it's about integration. You are not a collection of roles; you are a coherent whole.

Leadership built on that foundation doesn't just survive upheaval—it grows through it.

The Inner Conversation

The upcoming chapters invite you inward—exploring the unseen negotiations among emotion, identity, and purpose.

Emotional integrity teaches you to stay grounded when the world tries to pull you apart.

Cultural flexibility helps you navigate differences without losing empathy or self-respect.

Identity agility invites you to grow and evolve without erasing yourself in the process.

Together, these capacities make up The Mosaic Within—the living essence of composure.

Before leading others through conflict, you must reconcile your own. Every leader I've coached or observed faces the same invisible challenge: how to stay connected to themselves in systems that constantly demand compromise. The question is not if the world will test your alignment—it will. The real question is whether you'll remain emotionally fluent enough to notice when something within you starts to go silent.

That silence—the absence of inner dialogue—is where disconnection begins.

The Mosaic Within restores that conversation. It invites every part of you back to the table: the part that's tired, the part that's hopeful, the part that still believes. When these parts move in rhythm again, you stop reacting from fragmentation and start responding with coherence.

A Different Kind of Strength

We've been conditioned to judge strength by endurance — by how much you can carry, how long you can hold, and how steady you can appear while doing it. Leadership cultures across industries reward the leader who absorbs pressure without complaint, who stretches without breaking, and who pushes through every storm with a rigid kind of heroism. But endurance is only one form of strength — and often the least sustainable.

The Mosaic Within redefines strength as inner receptivity — the willingness to listen, especially to yourself. It's the ability to notice the quiet truths beneath the noise: the need for rest, the weight of unspoken emotion, and the cost of constant composure. This receptive strength doesn't contract; it expands. It helps you face pressure with awareness rather than resistance.

Composure without self-connection feels empty — like acting steady rather than genuinely experiencing it. But when your composure is based on emotional literacy, cultural empathy, and identity awareness, it becomes healing. It turns into a rhythm you return to, not a mask you wear. This internal change shifts composure from a demand to a practice — from something you "hold together" to something that holds you.

You no longer cling to appearing composed;
you breathe to maintain composure.
You no longer lead with armor;
you lead through awareness.

This is what The Mosaic Within offers — not a manual for perfection, not a strategy to suppress emotion, and not a script for appearing unshakeable. It teaches you how to stay whole when everything around you, and sometimes inside you, feels like it's falling apart. It gives you the tools to anchor your presence in truth rather than tension, in humanity rather than habit.

A different kind of strength appears — softer, steadier, more sustainable. A strength based not on endurance, but on alignment. A strength that doesn't break under pressure because it isn't built on pretending; it's built on understanding.

This is the strength of the modern leader: calm rooted in self-connection, clarity born from reflection, and composure that doesn't hide humanity — it shows it.

Reflection — Coming Home to Center

Before flipping the page, take a quiet inventory of your inner world:

- Where have you changed yourself so many times that you no longer recognize yourself?
- What part of yourself has gone quiet in the name of composure?
- What if leadership focused on authentic presence rather than managing perceptions?

Wholeness isn't a destination—it's a discipline.

It's the daily return to the parts of yourself that leadership once asked you to edit out.

That return begins here.

Welcome to *The Mosaic Within.*

Emotional Integrity: Staying Aligned When the World Pulls You Apart

Language Cue: Emotional Integrity

The alignment between what you feel, what you value, and how you lead — even when pressure tempts you to fracture.

From Fluency to Fidelity

In the last chapter, we discussed composure as emotional fluency — the ability to recognize, name, and navigate your internal emotions with clarity. Fluency is the foundation of emotional maturity because it helps you understand what's happening inside you. However, awareness alone isn't enough. You can become highly skilled at identifying your feelings and still act in ways that conflict with your core values. You can regulate your emotions, but you can still betray the parts of you that need honesty, courage, or boundaries. Fluency helps you interpret your inner world; fidelity ensures you honor it.

Emotional integrity is where awareness becomes responsibility — where fluency develops into consistency. It is the discipline of remaining faithful to who you are, even when pressure tries to draw you into old patterns or emotional shortcuts. Emotional integrity prevents composure from turning into a performance and turns calmness into credibility. It ensures that the steadiness people see outwardly is rooted in truth, not suppression, avoidance, or the desire to appear strong.

This marks the shift from managing your emotions to aligning with your true self. It's not about flawless behavior; it's about congruence — the quiet harmony between your values, emotions, and actions. When leaders act with emotional integrity, their composure becomes trustworthy. Their steadiness commands respect. Their presence says, "You can rely on me not just to stay calm, but to stay true to myself."

And that is true evolution: shifting from emotional fluency — the ability to understand yourself — to emotional fidelity — the dedication to live in a way that reflects your true understanding.

The Sound of Compromise

There are moments in every leader's life when you realize you've quietly drifted away from yourself. You're still performing, still producing, and still managing the choreography of expectations — but something inside feels slightly off-key. The words leaving your mouth sound right, but the echo inside doesn't match.

That subtle discord is the sound of compromised integrity — not the kind that makes headlines, but the invisible kind: the everyday fracture that occurs when you override your instincts, dilute your truth, or nod in agreement with something your conscience resists.

Emotional integrity connects your inner world with your outer leadership. It ensures that your calmness is authentic, not just for show. Without it, calmness becomes a fake mask that gradually suffocates the person wearing it.

Integrity is often viewed as moral or ethical conduct, but emotional integrity runs even deeper. It represents a state of inner harmony — a seamless connection between what you feel, what you value, and how you act. When these three align, you feel consistent. When they don't, you experience tension — a form of mental fatigue that drains quicker than any workload ever could.

The Subtle Forms of Self-Betrayal

Self-betrayal rarely happens suddenly. It sneaks in through small moments of quiet disconnection. You agree when your body says no. You downplay discomfort to keep the peace. You quiet your intuition because the room's noise feels louder than your inner voice. You act as if you don't see when a line is crossed — yours or someone else's — because pointing it out might cost you approval.

Each time this happens, you divide yourself into two: the person the world applauds and the one inside whispering, "This isn't me." Over time, that whisper fades into exhaustion. You lose clarity about what you truly believe because you've spent so much energy performing conviction instead of living it.

Value dissonance becomes the new normal, and your body suffers — through sleepless nights, clenched jaws, irritability, or emotional flatness. The tragedy is that self-betrayal often hides behind professionalism. You tell yourself you're being adaptable, collaborative, strategic. But adaptability without authenticity isn't composure — it's emotional erosion in disguise.

The Courage to Tell Yourself the Truth

The most difficult conversation a leader will ever have is with themselves. Emotional integrity starts there — in the sacred act of telling the truth without excuses or defenses. You can't align with what you refuse to admit.

It starts with small, unfiltered confessions: *I'm no longer inspired here. This meeting feels wrong. I'm pretending to be okay, but I'm not. I'm leading out of fear instead of conviction.*

Naming these truths doesn't make you weak; it makes you aware. Awareness is the first step of integrity. The moment you name what's real, you cease negotiating with what's false.

Honesty slows things down. It disrupts comfort, reveals tension, and invites discomfort from those who prefer illusion. But leaders who choose honesty over harmony are the ones who ultimately build trust. People might resist your truth initially, but they will always feel more secure with your integrity than your image.

When the World Pulls You Apart

We live in an age that values fragmentation. Success requires flexibility — until that flexibility turns into fracture. You assume different roles: confident on camera, diplomatic in meetings, empathetic at home, decisive during a crisis.

Without awareness, those parts of you stop communicating. You begin to feel like a mosaic that's been rearranged too many times — all the same pieces, but no longer creating a clear picture.

That's emotional misalignment — the subtle loss of internal rhythm. You're still high-functioning, but feeling hollow inside. You begin chasing validation instead of vitality, applause instead of alignment.

Every environment influences differently. Some reward compliance, others reward charisma. But unless you are anchored in awareness, you'll start mirroring each room's energy — shape-shifting into what's acceptable rather than what's authentic.

Composure requires a steady core. Emotional integrity is that core — the inner gravity that enables you to navigate differences without distortion. It's what keeps your leadership human when the world tries to make it cold or mechanical.

The Mirror Test

Here's the question that changes everything: *Can you look in the mirror and say, I am leading in alignment with what I believe — without flinching?*

If the answer is no, you're not failing — you're awakening. The mirror test isn't about shame; it's about seeing clearly. It reminds you that integrity rarely disappears in one decision — it gradually erodes.

Every time you notice the distance between intention and action, you're already starting to close it. Each decision and each silence either narrows or widens that gap.

Research from the University of Michigan's Ross School of Business shows that leaders who align with their expressed values experience greater well-being, stronger team bonds, and less burnout. The body's stress response actually decreases when actions align with beliefs. Integrity, it appears, isn't just ethical — it's a matter of physiological regulation.

Emotional integrity involves noticing the impact. It's not about being perfect; it's about staying close enough to your truth so you can still hear it, even when the noise around you gets loud.

Integrity Under Pressure

Pressure reveals what really matters. When stress increases, expectations tighten, and people let you down, or systems break, integrity faces its true test. It's easy to stay true when everything goes your way, but it's under fatigue and fear that maintaining integrity becomes an act of moral strength.

Under pressure, most leaders tend to swing between two extremes: over-control or over-compromise. Over-controllers tighten their grip—micromanaging and closing off empathy to keep order. Over-compromisers loosen boundaries—softening their stance and suppressing the truth to avoid conflict. Both reactions show a disconnection.

Emotional integrity takes a middle ground: presence — the ability to hold onto truth firmly while remaining relationally human. To say, *I disagree, but I still respect you.* To admit, *this is uncomfortable, but necessary.*

When you uphold integrity under pressure, you transform tension into grace. You stop reacting impulsively and start to shine — not because you never stumble, but because you never pretend.

Mosaic in Action: The Manager Who Chose Truth Over Harmony

During a high-stakes client presentation, a manager confidently advanced through her slides — until she reached a projection she knew was inflated. Her team had been under pressure to present aggressive numbers, and in the rush of preparation, no one challenged the optimism. Now, in front of senior stakeholders and a multimillion-dollar opportunity, she felt the familiar leadership tension: *stay silent and protect the moment, or speak up to safeguard the relationship.*

She felt the room's expectation pressing on her. The safer choice — or what seemed safe — was to keep going, finish the presentation, and address the discrepancy later. But she could sense the cost of silence. It would undermine her integrity, misrepresent her team, and create an unstable foundation for the partnership. So she took a breath, paused mid-slide, and said calmly, "Before we move on, I need to clarify a data point that doesn't match our current numbers. The projection here is outdated. Let me show you the most accurate version."

The room became quiet — not tense, but attentive. She explained the corrected figures, the assumptions behind them, and the risks they wanted the client to fully understand. When she finished, she anticipated disappointment. Instead, the lead stakeholder nodded and said, "Thank you. That actually tells me more about how you operate than any slide could."

Her honesty didn't threaten the deal; it strengthened it. The client later said that her willingness to correct the data openly showed stability, not weakness. They felt they could trust her leadership, her team, and the long-term partnership even more because she chose clarity over comfort.

This is emotional integrity in action — quiet, inconvenient, but unforgettable. It is the kind of truth-telling that builds trust, not because it is easy, but because it is rare.

The Cost of Compromise

Every leader can recall those moments when they stayed silent but shouldn't have. You remember the meeting where someone was dismissed, and you said nothing. The strategy you agreed to, even though it went against your values—the moment you chose peace over principle, comfort over clarity, belonging over truth. At the time, the choice felt necessary — the path of least disruption. But those moments stay with you. They resonate.

Compromise may seem small in the moment, but it leaves a mark inside. These moments don't just break confidence; they break clarity. You can't lead confidently while secretly regretting your silence. You can't influence with integrity when your inner voice feels ignored. Every unspoken truth becomes emotional residue — a weight you carry into the next conversation, decision, or version of yourself.

The cost of compromise isn't just external; it's internal. It gradually damages trust in your own judgment. It causes you to second-guess your instincts, hesitate in moments when you once acted decisively, and question whether your voice still matters. Leaders often mistake this erosion for self-doubt, but in reality, it stems from misalignment — a subtle fracture between who you are and how you show up.

The only way to restore integrity is through repair. And repair begins with acknowledgment:

That moment wasn't in line with who I am.

This is not self-blame; it is self-clarity. From that honesty, correction becomes possible. You start to see discomfort not as evidence of failure, but as feedback — a signal that your internal guidance system is alive and trying to steer you back into coherence.

When you reinterpret missteps as messages, you reclaim your power. You understand that integrity isn't maintained by perfection; it's built through continual adjustments. By noticing, naming, and choosing again, you learn to trust your tension — the quiet signal that something inside you is seeking alignment.

This is the core of emotionally mature leadership: not having a perfect record, but consistently returning to the truth. Not avoiding compromise, but being willing to correct course. Each time you recognize the cost of compromise, you build your ability for courageous clarity in the moments that come afterward.

Integrity develops not when everything is perfect, but when you choose to realign — again and again — with your true self.

The Mosaic of Alignment

Emotional integrity lies at the heart of The Mosaic Advantage™. It's the force that connects composure to authenticity. When your feelings, values, and actions align, you stop losing energy. You stop managing impressions and begin emanating coherence.

This alignment doesn't require constant serenity. It permits anger, uncertainty, and grief — as long as they're genuine. Integrity isn't about being agreeable; it's about being authentic.

People trust leaders who are consistent more than those who are flawless. When your presence remains steady regardless of pressure, you build relational integrity — the kind that fosters safety through sincerity, not performance.

Within The Mosaic Way™, emotional integrity is the foundation that supports every other ability. Without it, flexibility becomes weakness, and agility leads to fragmentation. When integrity anchors your core, you can stretch without breaking, evolve without losing yourself, and adapt without giving up who you are.

In that sense, emotional integrity is leadership equity—credibility that can't be bought, borrowed, or branded.

Repair and Realignment

When you notice misalignment, avoid the urge to shame yourself or to overcorrect. Shame hampers progress; overcorrection can distort it. Leaders often react to missteps by tightening up, defending, or doubling down — all of which increase the gap between intention and action.

The Mosaic Way™ offers a gentler, much more sustainable route.

Pause long enough to notice the dissonance.

That internal tightening, that subtle feeling of discord, is the body whispering, 'This isn't me.' Before analyzing, justifying, or intellectualizing, simply acknowledge the signal. Misalignment always speaks before it becomes visible.

Reflect on which values were overlooked or violated. Integrity cracks when needs are neglected—the need for rest, honesty, courage, and clarity. Misalignment follows self-abandonment. The question is not What went wrong? But what needs did I ignore that I didn't honor?

Repair by recalibrating.

This might involve starting a clarifying conversation, setting a boundary, sincerely apologizing, or changing a behavior to restore harmony. Repair is not flashy; it is steady. It realigns you with your truth and invites others back into trust.

When practiced this way, integrity becomes healing rather than punishment. It ceases to be an inflexible demand for perfection and becomes a continuous invitation into alignment — a steady, compassionate return to yourself. Leaders who embrace this rhythm foster emotional ecosystems where accountability feels secure, and growth feels attainable.

Why Alignment Feels Like Peace

When your inner world and outer actions finally align, something remarkable happens: peace.

Not the fragile kind that depends on perfect conditions, quiet environments, or unanimous agreement. But the resilient, steady kind born of coherence — the peace that comes from not being in conflict with yourself.

Peace isn't the absence of tension; it's the absence of contradiction.

You no longer have to perform calm; you *are* calm.

You no longer manage how others perceive you; your presence speaks for itself.

You no longer juggle competing identities; you embody a unified one.

Alignment quiets the internal friction that drains energy and erodes confidence. It frees up emotional bandwidth for creativity, connection, and clarity. It creates an inner spaciousness that others can feel, even before you say a word. This is what emotionally intelligent leadership sounds like at its purest: grounded, open, and unforced.

That is the essence of emotional coherence — the quiet strength of a leader whose integrity has become integrated. Composure stops being something you work to maintain; it becomes a natural extension of who you are. Because composure isn't about never bending, it's about knowing exactly where you stand, and standing there with steadiness and grace.

Reflection — Returning to Alignment

Before you finish this chapter, pause and ask yourself:

- Where am I saying yes to things that weaken my integrity?
- What value of mine have I sacrificed for belonging or approval?
- What would change if my composure reflected my truth instead of the mask that conceals it?

Emotional integrity is the quiet revolution that starts inside every calm leader. It's what keeps calm, honest, clarity, compassionate, and strength human.

You can't guide others back to alignment until you've walked that path yourself.

And when you do — when your calm finally reflects your convictions — you won't just appear composed.

You'll actually be composed.

In the next chapter, we'll explore what happens when your integrity encounters differences — how to lead across cultures, personalities, and pressures without losing empathy or context. Because composure doesn't end at alignment; it grows into understanding.

!

The Data That Demands Attention

Alignment between values and actions is not abstract—it is measurable. According to the 2024 Edelman Trust Barometer, 71 percent of employees say they will refuse to work for an organization that "acts inconsistently with its stated values." Among leaders, the gap between personal conviction and professional behavior is one of the top predictors of burnout. A 2023 Mind Share Partners report found that nearly half of executives who considered leaving their roles cited "ethical misalignment or loss of authenticity" as the primary reason.

Emotional integrity, therefore, is more than a virtue—it acts as a stabilizing force. Studies from the University of Oxford show that leaders who report high internal consistency demonstrate 23 percent greater decision confidence and higher resilience after organizational setbacks. The presence or absence of emotional integrity determines whether composure appears genuine or performative.

When the inner and outer selves are out of sync, exhaustion becomes unavoidable. The figures remind us that true calm starts with coherence—the bravery to live and lead from the same core.

A Word to the Generations

Generation X

You learned to compartmentalize—work here, life there, self somewhere in between. But the next era of leadership rewards integration. Let your steadiness tell one complete story.

Millennials

You've searched for purpose in your work for twenty years, often bearing the weight of meaning by yourself. Guard your alignment; it's not self-indulgence, it's endurance.

Generation Z

You resist hypocrisy instinctively. Use that conviction as a compass, not a weapon. Emotional integrity requires both honesty and humility.

Generation Alpha

You will grow up in a world obsessed with image. Remember: integrity is not what is seen, but what is maintained when no one watches.

Generation Beta

Your emotions will be measured, tracked, and analyzed. Integrity will mean trusting your internal signals even when algorithms suggest otherwise.

Which part of your generational voice feels strongest right now—clarity, connection, speed, or listening?

The Composed Practice

Composed — Chapter 4: Emotional Integrity

Truth · Coherence · Inner Alignment

I honor what I feel.
I live in alignment with my values.
My calm is genuine, not forced.

Take a slow breath in through your nose, then exhale through
your mouth.
Notice what softens when you stop pretending to be fine.
Integrity isn't about perfection; it's about presence that
tells the truth.

You have sacrificed parts of yourself to maintain peace.
But peace based on silence isn't truly peace—it's just
postponement.
Return to the voice within you that still knows what is true.

Place your hand over your heart and ask, 'Where have I said
yes when I meant no?' Do not rush to find the answer.
Just listen.
The moment you acknowledge what's real, alignment begins
to restore itself.

Calm is not compliance — it is clarity that breathes.
Stay honest enough to rest, and steady enough to begin
again.

Cultural Flexibility: Leading Without Losing Empathy or Context

Language Cue: Cultural Flexibility
The capacity to adapt across differences — not by abandoning yourself, but by expanding your understanding of others.

From Alignment to Connection

In the last chapter, we examined emotional integrity — the internal harmony between what you feel, what you value, and how you express yourself. Emotional integrity stabilizes your inner world. But alignment alone doesn't complete the picture. Leadership doesn't happen in isolation; it occurs in the presence of others whose maps of meaning differ from yours. Your composure may start with inner truth, but it matures through relationships.

This is where cultural flexibility comes into play — not as a performance, but as the genuine expression of integrity. It is empathy in action, the ability to remain true to yourself while making room for someone else's identity. It involves holding your own identity steady without dismissing the identities around you.

Cultural flexibility raises a deeper question: Can I stay true to myself while engaging with others on their level? Can I hold onto my values without dismissing yours?

Can I stay honest about my truth without diminishing yours?

Can I view behavior and communication through various perspectives, rather than only my own?

This represents a shift from alignment to connection. Moving from internal clarity to relational attunement. From "I understand myself" to "I understand how to show up for you without losing myself in the process."

Cultural flexibility doesn't require agreement, but it does demand awareness. It's the ability to recognize that tone, timing, expression, and emotional cues have different meanings across various identities and contexts. It's about the willingness to interpret rather than assume, to pause rather than react, and to adapt rather than insist.

When alignment meets connection, integrity transforms into influence. Your presence becomes not only focused but also expansive. People feel seen without being managed. They gain clarity without feeling controlled. And your leadership develops something rare: the ability to foster belonging without sacrificing selfhood.

This is the mosaic in motion — emotional integrity within, cultural flexibility without, and a leader who understands that composure is both a personal practice and a relational gift.

The Space Between Worlds

Leadership today exists in the space between worlds — across generations, departments, disciplines, values, and cultures. You might lead a team spanning three time zones, five languages, and seven belief systems. You could attend a meeting where one person measures success by profit, another by impact, and another by peace of mind.

This isn't chaos; it's the new reality. Navigating it requires more than policy or persuasion. It demands *cultural flexibility* — the emotional and cognitive agility to accept difference without defensiveness, to change perspective without losing integrity, to understand before asking to be understood.

Here's the truth most leaders resist: it isn't difference that drains us; it's disconnection. When you don't feel seen, when meaning slips through tone or translation, and when tension hums beneath every polite exchange, your nervous system starts leading the meeting before your mind arrives.

Cultural flexibility starts with *emotional literacy* — the ability to perceive not just spoken words but also unspoken feelings. It turns diversity from a checkbox into a meaningful conversation, and disagreement from a barrier into an opportunity for discovery.

Adaptation vs. Assimilation

Adaptation is a strength; assimilation is surrender. Too often, leaders blur the line between the two. They confuse flexibility with erasure — changing tone, language, or even posture to match the dominant style of the room. Over time, they become fluent in everyone else's culture but silent in their own.

True flexibility doesn't require you to disappear; it encourages you to expand. It involves translating your values instead of trading them. It's the difference between bending and breaking.

Assimilation says, *"I'll become whatever you need me to be."*

Adaptation says, *"I'll meet you where you are without losing where I stand."*

Cultural flexibility requires you to be both a mirror and an anchor—reflective enough to connect and grounded enough to stay genuine. Because when leaders lose themselves in translation, teams lose trust in their authenticity. And when authenticity disappears, psychological safety quickly falls apart.

Seeing Through Multiple Lenses

The most emotionally fluent leaders are not those who see the clearest, but those who see through many lenses. They understand that perspective shifts with position — that what seems obvious from one point of view may appear impossible from another.

To practice cultural flexibility, you need to rekindle curiosity. View assumptions not as facts but as opportunities for understanding. Ask, *"Tell me how you see it,"* and truly mean it.

That one sentence defuses defensiveness. It shows respect in environments where people have learned to armor themselves because their ideas are often misunderstood. When you create space for multiple truths, context comes into the conversation — and context changes everything.

Without context, behavior seems irrational. With context, behavior makes sense. A team member resisting change might not be stubborn; they could be scarred by numerous failed initiatives that cost good people their jobs. A colleague who avoids eye contact might not be detached; in their culture, sustained gaze is seen as aggression, not respect.

Cultural flexibility allows you to understand the human story behind people's actions.

Mosaic in Action — The Leader Who Listened Past Her Lens

During a global rollout meeting, a U.S. director led the discussion with her usual energy—asking open questions, setting clear expectations, and allowing plenty of space for dialogue. However, one thing unsettled her: the Asia-Pacific team remained silent. They nodded, took notes, and kept their cameras on, yet offered no opinions. Assuming their silence indicated agreement, she moved on. To her, participation meant speaking up. Silence, she believed, signified agreement.

Minutes after the meeting ended, a regional manager from Singapore sent a private message: "We're processing. In our culture, public disagreement shows disrespect. We need more time to respond thoughtfully." His message reframed the entire meeting. The director hadn't missed engagement — she had misinterpreted it. Her leadership perspective had filtered meaning through her own cultural norms: fast dialogue, verbal participation, and immediate reactions.

At the next session, she began with humility and clarity. "Last time, I mistook quiet for consent," she said. "Thank you for clarifying that for me. How can we structure our discussions so every voice — spoken or unspoken — feels heard and respected?" The change was immediate. The Asia-Pacific leaders offered suggestions: use pre-meeting prompts to help them prepare responses, dedicate time for written reflections, and rotate who speaks first so the pace doesn't favor one cultural style over another.

Participation soared. Conversations deepened. Trust grew. The team shifted from cautious cooperation to genuine collaboration. For the first time, every region felt equally valued — not because the director relinquished authority, but because she expanded her understanding of how authority could be shared.

Her flexibility wasn't a loss of leadership; it was an expansion of it. She showed emotional integrity by admitting her mistake, cultural flexibility by changing the meeting structure, and identity agility by tweaking her leadership style without giving up her core values.

That is *The Mosaic Way*™ in action — self-awareness engaging with cultural attunement, and leadership growing spacious enough for every voice to be heard.

When Empathy Becomes Exhausting

Empathy fatigue is real. The more you tune into the needs and histories around you, the easier it becomes to drown in understanding. You start to carry the weight of awareness instead of sharing it.

That's the paradox of modern leadership — we want emotionally intelligent leaders but seldom teach them how to manage empathy.

Unregulated empathy turns into overextension. You begin anticipating everyone's feelings, editing your truth to avoid discomfort, and confusing compassion with compliance.

Cultural flexibility remains sustainable only when grounded in boundaries. You can respect someone's story without taking on their emotions. You can listen intently without losing your balance. You can care without falling apart.

Empathy becomes strength when rooted in self-awareness and a strategy when combined with discernment.

Listening Across Difference

There are three kinds of listening:

- *Listening to respond* — hearing just enough to prepare a rebuttal.
- *Listening to relate* — translating everything through your own story.
- *Listening to understand* — suspending yourself long enough to perceive another's meaning.

Only the third creates a connection.

Listening across differences requires humility — the willingness to not be the loudest voice in the room; curiosity — the courage to replace certainty with learning; and composure — the steadiness to stay open when your worldview feels challenged.

The Mosaic Leader listens not for comfort but for context. They understand that discomfort isn't danger — it's data. It signals the edge of growth. When you listen that way, every conversation becomes a classroom.

Cultural Humility — The Quiet Discipline

Cultural humility isn't about perfecting protocols or memorizing greetings. It's about accepting that you will never fully understand another person's lived experience — and showing respect nonetheless. It is the practice of staying teachable, even when you are experienced. It is the awareness that every perspective, no matter how informed, still has blind spots.

Humble leaders don't just "include" others; they co-create a sense of belonging. They replace assumptions with inquiry and tokenism with trust. They don't wait for policies to mandate empathy — they embody it.

Cultural humility breaks down arrogance hidden as expertise. It reminds us that leadership isn't about mastering differences; it's about being guided by empathy.

Studies on cultural intelligence (Earley & Ang, Harvard Business Review, 2018) show that leaders who intentionally adapt communication across cultural contexts boost team performance and psychological safety by up to 35 percent. Flexibility isn't instinct; it's developed awareness — empathy turned into structure.

Leading in Translation

If emotional integrity is about alignment, then cultural flexibility is about translation — mastering the art of turning empathy into clarity and difference into understanding. Leaders who possess this skill are more than just communicators; they are bridge-builders. They interpret silence, reframe tone, and decode language — not only across dialects but also across generations, backgrounds, industries, and temperaments. They understand that every workplace contains multiple cultural worlds layered on top of one another, each with its own rhythms, norms, and emotional codes.

Translational leaders do not shy away from cultural tension; they approach it with curiosity rather than judgment. Instead of enforcing a single worldview — "Here's how we do things here" — they open pathways for shared understanding: "Help me understand what this means to you."

This simple shift changes everything. It signals respect. It communicates psychological safety. It expands what is possible in the relationship. And it honors the truth that diversity is not just demographic — it's cognitive, emotional, and experiential.

Translation is not dilution; it's amplification. It doesn't soften a message — it strengthens it by making sure it's received. A translated truth becomes a shared truth. When done well, translation expands reach without diluting clarity. It widens the circle without erasing the center. It turns leadership from a transactional exchange into a shared story — one where connection is the strategy and understanding is the goal.

In cross-cultural or cross-generational settings, translation is what separates influence from misinterpretation, unity from unspoken tension. The translational leader fosters spaces where people can be themselves, speak from their experience, and still feel part of something collective.

This exemplifies cultural flexibility in action — a leadership language that honors differences without losing focus. It is the point at which empathy becomes practical, communication becomes relational, and leadership becomes a vessel for belonging rather than authority.

Ultimately, leadership in translation isn't about saying more; it's about listening more deeply. It's the understanding that clarity is built together — not dictated — and that every voice, when truly heard, becomes part of the larger picture.

The Mosaic of Connection

Within The Mosaic Advantage™, cultural flexibility is the vital link that connects emotional integrity to identity agility. It acts as the connective tissue of modern leadership — a capacity that prevents integrity from becoming rigid and identity from falling into isolation. Without flexibility, integrity becomes rigidity, and identity becomes self-protection. But with it, diversity becomes synergy — a lively network where differences don't compete, but instead strengthen cohesion.

Cultural flexibility is more than interpersonal skill; it is a form of self-awareness that develops through relationships. It teaches you to lead not only across differences but through them. When you encounter another person's worldview, pace, or cultural rhythm, you start to rediscover yourself. You identify which parts of you stay vital regardless of the situation—your principles—and which parts are ready to grow—your perspective, assumptions, or emotional range.

Through this perspective, authenticity is not fixed. It develops over time. You become more truly yourself because of people unlike you. You see your identity more clearly because someone else perceives the world differently.

This is the core of cultural flexibility: it broadens your humanity without forcing you to dilute your truth.

When you're able to move easily between your principles and your perspective, between what grounds you and what challenges you, something shifts; you no longer feel the need to defend your difference. You stop clinging to sameness as a shield. You begin to embody your humanity — fluid, curious, open, and grounded.

That is the mosaic of connection — leadership that not only tolerates diversity but is transformed by it. It recognizes that difference is not an obstacle to coherence; it is a source of it. When integrity, flexibility, and agility come together, leaders don't lose themselves in the presence of others — they become more whole.

This is how Mosaic leaders foster cultures where belonging is not demanded but discovered, not forced but encouraged — a sense of belonging strengthened, not threatened, by diversity.

Composure in Cultural Conflict

Cross-cultural conflict is inevitable. The question isn't whether it happens, but how you handle yourself when it does. Cultural flexibility shifts conflict from being a threat to an invitation. Instead of defending your intent, focus on describing your impact. Instead of silencing discomfort, learn how to translate it.

When challenged, avoid the urge to correct automatically. Curiosity reconnects faster than justification. Ask, "What did you hear me say?" That single question reopens dialogue and shifts the energy from reactivity to reflection.

Composed leaders don't hurry to solutions; they focus on relationships. They know that understanding comes before agreement — and that being present helps resolve conflicts faster than trying to persuade. Such calmness turns friction into smoothness.

The Discipline of Perspective

Cultural flexibility is not just a mood; it's a discipline. It requires balancing paradoxes: confidence without arrogance, conviction without rigidity, and empathy without exhaustion. Within The Mosaic Way™, Cultural Flexibility exists between Emotional Integrity and

Identity Agility. Integrity keeps flexibility genuine; agility keeps it dynamic. Together, they create relational intelligence — the ability to navigate differences without losing oneself or exerting dominance.

The Mosaic Way reminds us that difference is never the enemy of calm — it is the mirror showing where calm is still conditional. Every cross-cultural encounter is a practice ground for being present. Pause before assuming. Connect before correcting. See before speaking. Live like that, and your leadership becomes multilingual at heart.

Reflection — Expanding Without Erasing

Pause and reflect:

- Where in my leadership do I adapt based on awareness rather than fear?
- Whose perspectives have I quietly ignored because they threatened my comfort?
- What would it look like to practice flexibility without losing my center — to lead with curiosity instead of control?

Cultural flexibility is the skill of staying true to humanity in translation — how we connect across generations, faiths, and borders.

In the next chapter, we'll explore what happens when that translation turns inward — how identity itself evolves through transition, belonging, and change because flexibility with others begins with agility within yourself.

!

The Data That Demands Attention

Cultural adaptability has become one of the most important predictors of leadership success. The World Economic Forum's 2025 Future of Jobs report ranks "cultural intelligence and empathy" among the top five global leadership skills for the next decade. However, despite increasing awareness, a 2024 McKinsey analysis found that only 29 percent of organizations actively train leaders to handle cultural or identity differences.

The costs of neglect are clear. Teams lacking cultural flexibility face a 32 percent higher rate of communication breakdowns and experience slower innovation cycles. In contrast, companies that focus on intercultural fluency see a 35 percent increase in team engagement and stronger problem-solving results. These findings show what human experience already proves: inclusion without understanding is fragile; empathy without skill is incomplete.

Cultural flexibility isn't about losing yourself — it's about expanding your capacity. In an age of interconnected pressures, leaders who can interpret difference without defensiveness create lasting belonging.

A Word to the Generations

Generation X — You built careers in environments that rewarded conformity. Now, your experience is needed to promote openness—showing that maturity and curiosity can coexist.

Millennials — You made inclusion a worldwide conversation. The next challenge is stamina: maintaining empathy when the process of understanding gets uncomfortable.

Generation Z — You challenge systems quickly and bravely. Remember that influence is strengthened through dialogue, not division. Being flexible makes your conviction more convincing.

Generation Alpha — You will inherit a borderless world. Let curiosity be your primary language. Your ability to adapt will decide not only where you belong but also how you lead.

Generation Beta — You will grow up globally connected. Flexibility will not be about blending in everywhere, but honoring difference without losing yourself.

- - - -- - - -

Which part of your generational voice feels strongest right now—clarity, connection, speed, or listening?

- - - -- - - -

The Composed Practice

Composed — Chapter 5: Cultural Flexibility

Empathy · Adaptation · Connection

I listen to understand, not to confirm.
I can bend without breaking.
Difference does not divide me—it expands me.

Pause before responding.
Feel the impulse to defend, then let it fade away. Curiosity
    isn't a weakness; it is wisdom dressed in humility.

You have been taught to lead with certainty.
But certainty can close things off. Flexibility, on the
    other hand, opens up space for meaning, nuance, and
    belonging that goes beyond sameness.

Place your hand over your heart and whisper, I can honor
    what is unfamiliar without losing myself.
Let that sentence expand your understanding, not your
    boundaries.

When you navigate differences with grace, you create bridges
    more resilient than mere agreement.
That is leadership—the art of translating through empathy.

Identity Agility: Becoming Without Breaking

Language Cue: Identity Agility
The capacity to evolve without erasing yourself — to adapt to new realities while remaining anchored in who you are.

From Flexibility to Fluidity

In the previous chapter, we discussed cultural flexibility — the skill of connecting across differences without erasing them. It's about expanding your understanding, adjusting your communication, and changing your perspective while staying true to yourself. But the most difficult translation isn't between cultures, generations, or worldviews. The toughest translation is the one within.

Identity agility occurs when you apply that same empathy inward — learning to evolve without abandoning your core self. It takes courage to release outdated versions of yourself while honoring the truths that still anchor you. It is the discipline of becoming without fracturing, expanding without dissolving, shifting without losing your shape.

Where cultural flexibility helps you navigate smoothly between external worlds, identity agility helps you move gracefully within your internal one. It is the quiet, ongoing process of negotiating between your past selves, your current reality, and the person you are intentionally becoming. It requires a different kind of strength —

not the strength to defend your identity, but the strength to revisit, question, and refine it.

Fluidity develops when you stop viewing identity as a fixed goal and start seeing it as a living system — responsive, adaptable, and deeply rooted. It isn't instability; it's responsiveness. It isn't self-abandonment; it's self-expansion. It allows you to hold multiple truths about yourself at once: who you have been, who you are becoming, and who you refuse to stop being.

This is the shift from flexibility to fluidity — from managing differences around you to embracing transformation within you. It is the practice of becoming while staying whole.

When the Mirror No Longer Matches

There comes a point in every leader's journey when you look at your reflection — in a literal mirror or in the eyes of those you lead — and notice a subtle dissonance. The posture has shifted. Edges have softened in some areas and sharpened in others. You are familiar, but not quite the same.

That moment is not a crisis; it's an awakening.

Identity agility starts with honest acknowledgment that transformation isn't betrayal. It's a continuous balancing act between staying the same and embracing change. In a world that moves faster than we can think, many leaders hold onto outdated versions of themselves, confusing consistency with integrity. But true integrity is flexible: you stay true to your values even as you express them differently.

Identity agility doesn't ask you to abandon who you've been; it asks you to integrate who you're becoming. You gather every chapter and say, *This, too, is me.*

The Myth of the Fixed Self

Leadership culture has long valued the steady hand — the unwavering figure whose certainty never falters. In complex systems, rigidity pretending to be strength becomes fragility. The self is not a monument; it's a river. It carries memory but must flow to stay alive.

Identity agility challenges the myth of a fixed self. New contexts reshape your sense of role, voice, and belonging. The real danger is not change itself, but resisting it until you break. When you insist on remaining who you once were for a stage that no longer exists, composure becomes performance. You cling to scripts that no longer suit the scene.

The Mosaic Way™ reminds us: identity isn't a costume to wear; it's a current to navigate. You're not supposed to stay still — you're meant to move with awareness.

Evolution Without Erosion

Adaptation becomes unhealthy when it sacrifices authenticity. Many leaders stumble here, confusing change with loss of core values. You can update methods, language, and style without losing your essence. The key is remaining connected to emotional integrity — the inner guide that directs you as external changes occur.

Ask: *Which parts of me are negotiable, and which are non-negotiable?*

Your methods should evolve. Your mission should deepen. Your values — the anchors of your truth — must stay intact.

Evolution that preserves its core creates wisdom. Evolution that forsakes its core leads to burnout. Identity agility is the ability to recognize differences.

The Pressure to Rebrand

Organizations reward reinvention — agility, disruption, innovation — but rarely consider the psychological toll of continuous pivots. Each change requires a new narrative. Every promotion calls for a new stance. Over time, you might lose sight of what was genuine and what was strategic. *Quiet rebranding fatigue* begins to set in: constantly changing, never feeling settled.

Identity agility promotes a slower, more authentic pace of change. It's not about marketing yourself into relevance; it's about maturing into resonance. When evolution arises from alignment rather than anxiety, people can notice the difference. Your growth shifts from appearing frantic to sounding like genuine becoming.

Mosaic in Action — The Leader Who Chose Resonance Over Relevance

After twenty years climbing the ranks of a global brand, a senior executive left a role others saw as the peak of success. Her departure left colleagues confused. They called it a pivot, a risk, even a professional gamble. But she saw it differently. "I kept calling it a pivot," she said, "until I realized it was a reconciliation." Over the years, she had shaped her tone, pace, and presence to fit the demands of a fast-changing corporate world. She had learned to soften her empathy to seem more efficient and to suppress her intuition so it wouldn't disrupt momentum. Her influence increased, but her resonance lessened. She was relevant in every room — but not reflected in any of them.

Launching a social-impact venture wasn't a reinvention; it was a return. She wasn't abandoning her past — she was integrating it. She carried forward her strategic rigor, operational expertise, and global perspective, but she reclaimed the parts of herself she had muted to succeed. "I didn't leave to become someone new," she said. "I left to stop abandoning who I already was."

What happened next surprised even her. Instead of shrinking, her influence grew. Her voice became clearer. Her impact deepened. People followed her not because of her title, but because of her authenticity. Investors trusted her vision. Partners were drawn to her clarity. Young leaders sought her mentorship, attracted to the steadiness she projected. Her leadership didn't weaken outside the corporate structure — it became more captivating.

Her story exposes a truth many leaders overlook: agility may seem risky on the surface but feels rewarding internally. Identity agility isn't about running away; it's about merging — aligning purpose with pace, impact with integrity, and ambition with authenticity. When she stopped twisting herself to stay relevant, she became impactful. And impact, unlike relevance, lasts.

That is what identity agility looks like: growth that respects your history, amplifies your humanity, and brings you home to yourself while opening up new possibilities for others.

The Agility of Belonging

At its core, identity agility is about belonging — not the kind granted, negotiated, or approved by others, but the kind you learn to grant yourself. Belonging, in its purest form, is adaptable. It develops as you grow, move, question, heal, and change roles. Still, many of us tie our sense of belonging to external structures: a title that affirms our competence, a community that reflects our identity, a culture that once acknowledged our worth. When those external signals fade or shift, it can feel like displacement — a quiet exile from the spaces that once felt like home.

But exile, properly understood, is not always a wound. Sometimes, it is a sacred threshold—a corridor between who you were and who you are becoming. A space where the noise of expectation quiets long enough for you to hear the voice you forgot was yours. Exile reveals the gap between borrowed belonging and the belonging that grows from within.

The Mosaic Way™ redefines belonging not as attachment to a place, role, or approval system but as alignment with purpose, identity, and presence. Belonging becomes less about fitting in and more about recognition — the internal acknowledgment of who you are, what you carry, and how you navigate the world. It is the shift from "Do they accept me?" to "Am I aligned here?"

Being identity-agile means trusting that you can belong anywhere when you bring full awareness. When your presence is integrated—emotionally honest, culturally attuned, and rooted in self-understanding—you stop searching for entry points. Instead, you create them. You stop waiting for permission to exist and start inhabiting your life with authority.

Home, then, is not a place. It is not a group. It is not a role.

Home travels with you — in the integrity of your presence, the clarity of your purpose, and the fidelity you hold to your own becoming. When you lead from that place, belonging is no longer something you chase; it becomes something you embody.

Identity agility is the courage to carry your home with you, even as the world changes around you. It is the leadership ability that turns movement into meaning, transition into truth, and uncertainty into coherence.

Organizations With a Soul

What is true of people is also true of systems. Organizations break apart when they hold onto an origin story without updating it for today. "This is who we've always been" turns into dogma. Identity-flexible organizations act differently. They respect history but do not idolize it. Culture becomes a living ecosystem instead of a museum. The key question shifts from How do we protect what was? to How do we stay true to our core while remaining relevant to the times?

These organizations enable people to articulate the mission in their own language and through their own identities. Structures come alive. Feedback shapes them without destroying them. In such systems, people no longer have to choose between authenticity and progress; they develop within the organization without feeling they need to leave it behind.

The Inner Split

Without identity agility, an inner split occurs. You start living two stories simultaneously — the outer narrative that seeks approval and the inner narrative that searches for truth. Over time, the gap between them becomes too much to bear. You feel like an imposter, not because of a lack of skill, but because you've outgrown your shell.

The solution isn't to destroy your life; it's to bridge the divide. Bring your public and private selves into conversation. Ask: *What am I hiding to stay accepted?* Then ask: *What would happen if I stopped hiding it?*

Identity agility develops from honesty. It's not about rejecting the old self, but about combining it with the new with compassion. Authenticity isn't a comeback; it's an expansion.

Agility as Emotional Architecture

Identity agility is both psychological and physiological. It changes how the body responds. Every transition — whether it's a new team, new tool, or new culture — is stored in the nervous system. If you don't process the emotional data of transition, your body stays tense even after the change is over.

Composed leaders engage in micro-resets — breathing, reflection, brief pauses — signaling to the system: I am safe to grow. Agility requires safety; safety depends on awareness. In this way, composure becomes the foundation that supports your evolving identity — grounded enough to adapt, flexible enough to remain whole.

Neuroscience confirms this connection. The brain's anterior cingulate cortex — which handles blending emotion and decision-making — becomes active during mindful identity reflection. According to the Harvard Center for Positive Organizational Scholarship (2022), leaders who engage in reflective identity work during transitions report 40 percent higher resilience and retention. Agility isn't a personality trait; it's a trained neuro-emotional skill.

The Paradox of Reinvention

You cannot become new without honoring the old. Reinvention is not an escape from your past but an evolution shaped by it. Many people try to sprint away from earlier versions of themselves — embarrassed by their choices, protective of their missteps, or impatient with the parts of their identity that no longer fit. But every former self served a purpose. Each identity was built for its season. Every version protected something you weren't yet ready to lose or weren't yet equipped to face.

Identity-agile leaders understand this. They view former versions of themselves as teachers, not ghosts. They can say, "*I needed that armor once; now I can put it down.*" They recognize that survival strategies were smart responses to earlier environments — and that true maturity involves not rejecting them, but releasing them with gratitude.

Reinvention that respects history builds resilience. It enables you to learn from the past without carrying old wounds into new spaces, allowing you to evolve with continuity rather than fragmentation. When you honor the purpose your previous identities served, you strengthen the foundation of your current confidence.

Reinventing oneself by dismissing the past, however, leaves you unmoored. It pretends that history doesn't repeat itself, that emotional memory doesn't influence behavior, and that discarded identities won't resurface under pressure. Without honoring where you've been, the future becomes a performance rather than genuine growth.

The paradox is this: you grow best when you integrate your history, not when you ignore it. Growth demands both evolution and remembrance — the courage to move forward and the humility to look back. Identity agility is the ability to carry your past wisely, your present clearly, and your future freely.

The Mosaic of Becoming

Within The Mosaic Way™, Identity Agility completes the triad. Emotional Integrity keeps you honest. Cultural Flexibility keeps you connected. Identity Agility keeps you evolving. Together, they form the leadership rhythm of coherence → connection → creation.

Every identity is a mosaic — pieces of experience, culture, relationships, loss, and triumph — held together not by sameness but by intention. Identity agility is the permission to reassemble those pieces as life demands without losing the essence of who you are.

In practice, this means giving yourself permission to outgrow roles that once defined you. It involves allowing the edges of your identity to breathe—embracing new colors and shapes. You don't lose wholeness when you change; you only lose it if you refuse to.

When identity is seen as a mosaic, composure ceases to be static. It becomes alive — a constantly changing balance between memory and movement.

Micro-Practice — The Identity Scan

Take sixty seconds. List three words that described you five years ago and three that describe you now. Notice the continuity and the contrast. Which words have become part of your permanent makeup — traits that stay true regardless of role or season? Which words no longer fit, not because you failed them but because you outgrew the environments that once required them?

This practice isn't about nostalgia; it's about clarity. Awareness comes before agility. When you recognize the identities that have remained, shifted, or softened, you can navigate change with purpose. The scan reveals a simple truth: transformation doesn't erase who you are — it refines who you've always been.

The Future Belongs to the Fluid

The next era of leadership will belong to those who can move— across disciplines, across differences, across identities—without losing their center. As work becomes more global, more virtual, more complex, and more emotionally demanding, rigidity will not protect leaders; it will fracture them. Adaptability is no longer a competitive advantage. It is the psychological literacy needed to navigate disruption with coherence rather than collapse.

Identity agility is the new leadership fluency. It is the ability to shift without changing your core, to evolve without losing yourself, to expand without becoming unrecognizable. Teams today need leaders who can interpret context, understand nuance, communicate across cultures, and adapt their presence without sacrificing their integrity.

Those who cannot adapt without losing themselves will break under rapid change. Their teams will follow. But leaders who can stay grounded and flexible — steady and gentle, anchored and adaptable — will foster cultures strong enough to stretch, grow, and recover. They become stabilizing forces in environments where everything else is in motion.

Fluid leaders do not fear change; they understand it. They do not resist evolution; they lead through it. Because they know who they are, they can meet others where they're at. That is the future of leadership: not certainty, but coherence. Not control, but alignment. Not perfection, but presence.

Reflection — Evolving With Integrity

Pause and reflect:

- Where am I holding onto a version of myself that no longer fits the current situation?
- What part of me has been waiting for permission to change?
- How can I stay flexible without losing my authenticity — improving my methods while safeguarding my core?

Identity agility isn't about constant change; it's about conscious change — the discipline of evolving without breaking, growing without losing oneself, expanding without erasing. Practice it, and composure stops feeling like control and begins to feel like freedom.

You no longer defend who you once were.

You embrace who you are now — fully, fluidly, fearlessly.

In the chapters ahead, we'll shift from focusing on the individual to the collective — exploring how identity-agile leaders build organizations and cultures that grow at the same rate as their people. The Mosaic Way™ doesn't end with personal coherence; it starts there. From that core, everything else learns how to move.

!

The Data That Demands Attention

Identity has become a shifting target in modern leadership. According to a 2024 Pew Research Center study, 64 percent of professionals say they have "redefined their personal or professional identity" in the past five years due to changing roles, values, or environments. The World Health Organization identifies "identity strain" as an emerging factor in workplace stress—especially among leaders managing hybrid teams and cross-generational expectations.

A 2023 MIT Sloan Management Review analysis revealed that organizations promoting authentic self-expression experience a 47 percent increase in innovation and better retention among younger employees. However, nearly half of executives still admit to "masking aspects" of their true selves to meet expected norms. This disconnect between adaptation and authenticity causes emotional exhaustion—the gradual depletion of energy needed to maintain a divided self.

The data confirms a timeless truth: agility isn't about changing who you are to survive, but about expanding who you are to lead. When identity remains flexible without breaking apart, composure shifts from mere endurance to mastery.

A Word to the Generations

 **Generation X** You were taught to hold onto one idea of success. But life has asked you to reinvent yourself over and over. Let reinvention feel like wisdom, not failure.

 **Millennials** You have mastered the art of the pivot—shifting careers, values, and identities. Embrace that adaptability, but remember that groundedness isn't rigidity; it's rhythm.

 **Generation Z** You live in a culture of constant self-definition. Protect your sense of self from the performative aspect of it. Identity agility means staying true to yourself even as you evolve.

 **Generation Alpha** You will grow up connected to every voice, label, and perspective. Let that connection expand your empathy without erasing who you are. You belong, even as you change.

 **Generation Beta** You will be encouraged to reinvent constantly. Identity agility will mean evolving by addition—not erasure.

Which part of your generational voice feels strongest right now—clarity, connection, speed, or listening?

The Composed Practice

Composed — Chapter 6: Identity Agility

Evolution · Wholeness · Self-Trust

I can change without losing who I am. I am allowed to grow
beyond what once defined me.
I evolve, not to please others, but to fulfill my own
becoming.

Pause for a moment and observe who you've been trying
to be.
Feel the tension between expectation and your true self. Let
go of the versions of you that once served you—they
were never mistakes, only stages of growth.

You don't owe anyone your old self.
Authenticity isn't about repetition; it's about renewal.
Each phase of your life deserves its own expression.

Place your hand over your heart and whisper, I am still me,
even when I'm new.
Let that truth loosen the armor of who you were supposed
to be.

Agility isn't instability—it's integrity in motion.
You aren't losing form; you're taking shape.

PART III _____

The Language of Calm

Language Cue: Expression

The outward translation of inner alignment — how calm becomes communicable.

Composure Speaks

Composure isn't silence. It communicates — through tone, timing, and presence.

It's the look that calms a room before a word is spoken, the pause that prevents a meeting from breaking apart, the phrase that eases defensiveness without weakening truth.

By now, you've completed the interior work. You've restored emotional integrity, grown through cultural flexibility, and moved with identity agility. You've built the internal structure of wholeness.

Now, the question is: *How does that sense of wholeness sound?*

Leadership is measured not only by what you know or decide, but also by the emotional climate you foster when you speak.

The composed leader doesn't just communicate information — they also convey regulation. Their language slows down what's rushing, grounds what's reactive, and reconnects what's been torn apart.

This is *The Language of Calm* — leadership as emotional translation in action.

The Voice Beneath the Voice

Every leader speaks two languages: the language of words and the language of energy. You can deliver the perfect phrase and still create tension if your energy conflicts with your intent. You can say very little and still reassure a team if your presence conveys safety.

That's the paradox of composure — it's more about vibration than vocabulary. When you speak from inner coherence, people feel calmness. They might not understand why, but something inside them exhales.

Most communication training emphasizes clarity, persuasion, or confidence. Mosaic communication introduces a deeper layer: *congruence.*

It's not just what you say but the state you're in when you say it.

This is where emotional awareness becomes audible — where words serve as tools for safety or stress. Composed leaders learn to listen to the underlying frequency beneath their own voice.

The Weight of Words

Under pressure, words carry more weight. People rarely listen to what you actually say; they hear what they need to hear from you. In high-stress situations, language becomes a crucial part of leadership. A careless remark can cause division; a thoughtful statement can rebuild trust.

Composed leaders recognize that calm isn't silence — it's purposefulness. They speak slowly enough to think, clearly enough to be understood, and softly enough to be felt. Their words don't demonstrate authority; they embody it.

They don't rush to fill silence; they honor it.

They don't minimize pain; they acknowledge it with dignity.

That's how calm travels — through sentences that restore safety instead of reinforcing control.

Boundaries and Belonging

Boundaries and belonging are not opposites — they are partners in stability. Too often, leaders think they must choose between clarity and compassion. But true emotional intelligence recognizes that structure and safety are related — one protects, the other nurtures.

Boundaries expressed with clarity and warmth convey: *This space matters. You matter. And I matter, too.* They uphold dignity on all sides. In "Boundaries That Protect Belonging," we examine how composed leaders foster cultures where empathy doesn't lead to exhaustion and openness doesn't descend into chaos. Boundaries are not barriers to inclusion — they're the language that sustains inclusion.

The Rhythm of Restoration

Composure isn't fixed; it's rhythmic. No one remains centered all the time. Even the most grounded leaders lose their rhythm — what matters is how quickly and gently they recover. In a world addicted to noise, restoration becomes a radical act. It involves choosing reflection over reaction, pause over performance, and presence over perfection.

Composure isn't built in stillness; it's tested in motion. Restoration is what keeps it alive. When you restore your rhythm, you demonstrate resilience. You teach that steadiness doesn't require suppression and that leaders can recover without retreating.

That's the mature language of calm — not avoidance, but alignment.

The Mosaic in Motion

By this point, the Mosaic is no longer just a framework — it's a rhythm you live by. Emotional integrity provides your compass. Cultural flexibility builds your bridge. Identity agility gives you wings.

Now, your composure shifts. Leadership becomes less about control and more about coherence — less about directing others and more about designing emotional space in real time.

When you speak with alignment, your words become architecture. They encompass the emotional structure of the moment — shaping uncertainty, providing context to conflict, and establishing rhythm for renewal.

That's what *The Language of Calm* really is: emotional design in action.

Reflection — Speaking from the Center

Pause and ask yourself:

- When I speak under pressure, do my words reflect my values or my fears?
- Do I use language to evoke calm or to establish calm?
- What does my tone communicate when my silence cannot?

You don't need perfect phrasing; you need authentic presence.

Because leadership isn't only seen — it's felt.

And in a world still learning how to listen, your calm may be the clearest language anyone hears.

CHAPTER 7 ———————————

When Words Steady the Room

Language Cue: Regulation
The power to calm, clarify, and connect through presence in speech.

From Inner Agility to Outer Alignment

In the last chapter, we discussed identity agility — the internal flexibility that lets you evolve without losing yourself. It's the quiet inner work of staying honest, grounded, and adaptable as your circumstances change. But integrity, no matter how strongly held, must eventually speak up. At some point, your internal alignment has to move from the privacy of your thoughts into the shared space of other people's nervous systems.

Composure becomes visible when it is expressed aloud. It is most clearly recognized not by what you feel internally, but by how you communicate those feelings. Here, regulation acts as the bridge — the moment when inner calm translates into outer stability, when your internal coherence becomes something others can sense, hear, and trust.

The Mosaic Way™ teaches that leadership maturity is judged not just by what you feel, but by how your words affect others. Your tone acts as a transmission. When your voice aligns with your intention, the room naturally gathers around it. People feel more secure, clearer, and more grounded in your presence. If your voice carries agitation, the room absorbs it. Confusion spreads. Anxiety increases. Even if your content is accurate, your delivery can still cause harm.

Regulation isn't about suppressing emotion or appearing neutral. It's about channeling energy into coherence—selecting language, pacing, and presence that mirror your values rather than your impulses. It involves guiding your emotions instead of letting them spill out. When inner agility aligns with outer balance, your composure becomes not just an internal achievement but a way to connect with others. Your presence does more than hold you together; it also helps hold the space around you.

The Moment Before You Speak

There is always a pause — however brief — before a leader's words enter the world. In that small, sacred space, everything hangs in balance: tension, trust, and tone. Most people rush to fill that silence, afraid of the discomfort it causes. Yet the composed leader understands that silence is not absence; it is architecture. It's the place where intention takes shape, where awareness has a chance to catch up with emotion.

Speech starts in the diaphragm before it reaches the mouth — how you breathe influences the atmosphere of the room. What you choose to release after that pause determines whether the room escalates or relaxes. Words are never neutral; they carry energy. They either amplify emotion or absorb it.

When you speak from reactivity, your language acts as a catalyst, fueling anxiety or defensiveness. When you speak from alignment, it becomes a steadying force that grounds others in coherence. The difference isn't eloquence or charisma; it's self-regulation. Composed leaders regulate themselves before they communicate. They breathe first, then speak. Their pause is not hesitation — it is calibration.

Tone: The Temperature of Trust

Tone conveys more than vocabulary ever can. You can say "I'm listening" in a way that invites truth — or in a way that warns against it. You can apologize in a way that heals — or in a way that simply ends the conversation.

Neuroscience reveals that tone is processed more quickly than meaning; the body reacts before the brain interprets. This explains why a team perceives your state long before they understand your message. Studies in affective neuroscience (Van der Kolk & Porges, 2021) demonstrate that vocal tone and pacing directly influence listeners' vagal response, reducing collective stress within sixty seconds. In other words, your tone physically alters physiology.

The Mosaic Way™ describes tone as emotional temperature. A warm tone fosters connection and shows receptivity. A cool tone creates distance and signals caution. A neutral tone provides a safe space where neither defensiveness nor intensity dominates.

The composed leader monitors this temperature precisely. They understand that calm is not monotony; it's measured — a balance of strength and softness, gravity and grace. Tone is where composure becomes audible, and it's often the first language trust recognizes.

Timing: When Clarity Waits

In high-pressure settings, urgency often hides as importance. Leaders might confuse activity with progress, thinking that quicker communication will ease anxiety. But staying calm brings courage to timing — the courage to wait until clarity appears.

Words spoken too early turn into noise, scattering understanding before it can take hold. Words spoken too late, however, leave silence to harden into resentment or confusion. Leadership requires the ability to read the emotional flow and speak when the moment is most receptive.

Experienced leaders practice what The Mosaic Way™ calls temporal empathy — an attunement not only to what people need to hear, but also to when they are ready to hear it. They pause before correction, allowing emotion to settle. They debrief after tension eases, ensuring that instruction lands on stable ground. Timing, when guided by empathy, transforms communication from command into connection and turns instruction into insight.

Mosaic in Action — When a Leader's Voice Became the Anchor

During a hospital-wide emergency drill, alarms blared throughout the corridors, monitors flashed red, and team leaders shouted conflicting instructions. What was supposed to be a simulation quickly turned into a wave of real panic. Nurses rushed in different directions, residents talked over each other, and fear spread faster than the protocol meant to contain it. The medical director watched the room's emotional temperature rise — not because people lacked competence, but because their nervous systems had taken control of the situation.

She moved forward, raised her hand, and spoke into the chaos with a quiet but clearly steady voice: "One breath at a time." She didn't shout. She didn't demand. She simply lowered her tone until it became impossible not to follow. Within seconds, shoulders relaxed. Conversations softened. The overwhelming layering of voices faded into focused cooperation. People found their place again — not because the challenge disappeared, but because her calmness gave them something solid to align with.

After the drill, a nurse pulled her aside. "It wasn't what you said," she told her. "It was how you said it. Your calm became ours." The medical director realized she hadn't just directed the room; she had regulated it. Her nervous system had become the anchor for dozens of others.

This is regulation at its purest — composure as transmission, not performance. It's the kind of leadership that steadies others because you have already steadied yourself. In moments of chaos, words matter. But tone matters more. Presence does the work before language ever arrives.

Truth: The Anchor in Ambiguity

Calm does not mean avoidance. In fact, avoidance breeds the very anxiety that composure is meant to resolve. When pressure increases, people crave honesty more than reassurance. Yet, truth without tenderness can break, and tenderness without truth can deceive. The composed leader understands this paradox. They speak truth in a way that maintains dignity, balancing honesty with compassion.

Instead of rushing to fix discomfort, they express it clearly. A helpful rhythm for honesty looks like this: name reality ("This change is difficult"), name emotion ("You may feel uncertain or frustrated"), and name intention ("Our goal is clarity, not perfection"). This simple trio stabilizes both sides. It tells the nervous system: We are seen. We are safe. We are in the process.

Truth, when spoken with composure, becomes the anchor that keeps the team steady amid ambiguity.

Words as Containment

In moments of crisis, people don't just want answers — they want containment. They seek someone whose words can hold what feels unholdable. Containment doesn't lessen fear; it organizes it. It provides language strong enough to carry what emotion cannot express.

When a composed leader says, "Let's take this one step at a time," they're not offering a cliché — they're restoring order to chaos. When they say, "We can pause here before we decide," they're reinstating agency.

Containment language has rhythm: short, grounded sentences, a low emotional pitch, and clear next steps. It sounds steady because it is steady. Through that rhythm, a leader's words control the room. This is why composure is contagious — language spreads regulation the same way heat spreads light, transferring coherence from one person to another until the environment calms.

Micro-Practice — The 60-Second Centering Script

Before a high-stakes conversation, spend a moment to align your body and presence.

Step 1: Pause and take four slow, deep breaths. **Step 2:** Ask yourself three grounding questions:

- What matters most right now?
- What tone builds trust?

- Which single sentence propels us forward?

Step 3: Speak only after your breath and body align with your intention. This demonstrates verbal composure in motion — regulation as leadership.

The Courage to Be Understood

Most leadership communication secretly hides a worry: *What if they misunderstand me?* This fear often leads to over-explaining, defensiveness, or trying to control the message. But maintaining composure removes the need to control how others interpret. Instead, it focuses on clarity — making sure that intent and delivery align, even if not everyone agrees with the message.

When your words mirror your values, clarity naturally follows. The Mosaic Leader speaks to be understood, not to seek approval. They understand that transparency may cause discomfort, but they also see that discomfort isn't danger — it's the first language of growth.

Calm communication doesn't weaken conviction; it expresses it clearly, turning possible tension into trust through authenticity.

The Rhythm of Repair

Even the most grounded leaders make mistakes or misread a situation. What sets them apart is how quickly and humbly they correct themselves. Repair is the language of accountability; it restores trust in relationships after a rupture.

A composed apology sounds like this: *"That didn't come out how I intended,"* or *"I can see how that landed differently for you,"* or *"Let's reset and clarify."* These phrases share a common rhythm — ownership, empathy, and re-engagement. No defensiveness. No dramatics. Just presence.

Repair doesn't eliminate imperfection; it normalizes humanity. In doing so, it shows everyone around you that calm isn't the absence of error but the presence of recovery. This rhythm of repair is what transforms communication into connection and mistakes into momentum.

When Your Silence Speaks

There are moments when words can't stabilize the room — times of grief, loss, or deep conflict. In those moments, presence becomes the message. Composed silence isn't withdrawal; it's witness. It says, *I'm here. I see this. I'm not afraid of it.*

The Mosaic Way™ describes this *anchored silence* as the kind that holds space without rushing to fill it. It conveys safety through breath, eye contact, and posture. Anchored silence shows others that not everything fragile needs fixing and that some truths are best respected rather than controlled. Sometimes, the most powerful statement you can make is to stand still and let truth breathe.

The Mosaic of Communication

When emotional integrity guides your tone, cultural flexibility informs your timing, and identity agility shapes your expression, your communication becomes a mosaic. Every word reflects coherence. Every pause respects differences. Every message carries the full weight of who you are.

Within The Mosaic Way™, regulation is where the inner and outer mosaic come together — emotional integrity provides honesty, cultural flexibility offers empathy, and identity agility gives it voice. Regulation completes the cycle by transforming inner alignment into outer resonance.

This is where composure moves from theory to reality — when your language no longer symbolizes calm, but actually creates it. Composed communication doesn't merely share thoughts; it offers safety. It shifts leadership from merely performance to genuine presence and turns conversation into a meaningful connection.

Reflection — Speaking from Stillness

Pause and ask yourself:

- When pressure increases, do my words align with the problem or the solution?
- How do I use silence — as withdrawal or as wisdom?
- What tone would I want to hear if I were on the other side of my own leadership?

Your words reflect your composure. When they bring stability to a room, they remind others that calmness isn't the absence of challenge — it's the mark of true leadership. And during uncertain times, that kind of presence becomes a powerful force.

In the next chapter, we shift from individual speech to collective resonance — exploring how language, tone, and presence ripple through entire cultures. The Mosaic Way™ refers to this next phase as "The Atmosphere of Leadership" — the space where regulated individuals build emotionally intelligent systems.

!

The Data That Demands Attention

In moments of stress, language acts as the first stabilizer—or the initial spark. A 2024 MIT Human Dynamics Lab study found that tone and pacing make up to 83 percent of how a message is interpreted under pressure, surpassing word choice itself. The Harvard Center for Public Leadership reports that teams led by communicators who maintain a calm, clear tone see a 31 percent improvement in crisis decision-making compared to those led by reactive communicators.

Yet, communication fatigue is increasing. According to Microsoft's 2024 Work Trend Index, the average professional receives over 120 digital messages daily, and attention spans have shrunk by nearly 25 percent in the past decade. The result is a leadership environment where calm speech has become an act of defiance—and influence is shaped not only by what is said but also by how it is delivered.

The evidence is clear: composed language doesn't silence urgency; it channels it. In an age of acceleration, the leader who can steady a room with words becomes the one people trust to guide it forward.

A Word to the Generations

 You came of age in cultures that value direct communication—decisive, clear, efficient. Now your task is translation: balancing authority with empathy so that clarity doesn't feel cold.

 You formed connections through conversation, even amid chaos. Guard that instinct, but ground it in discipline. Words can comfort or clutter; select the few that foster calm.

 You communicate across platforms quicker than any previous generation. Your strength is in your intention. Let your tone convey as much awareness as your message.

 You will inherit a world of immediate dialogue. Understand early that influence starts with listening. The quietest voice in the room often contains the most truth.

 Your words will travel fast. Let them land gently. Calm will become your most influential language.

Which part of your generational voice feels strongest right now—clarity, connection, speed, or listening?

The Composed Practice

Composed — Chapter 7:
When Words Steady the Room

Language · Resonance · Presence

My words shape what I believe.
My tone reflects my truth.
I speak to guide, not to control.

Before you speak, pause.
Notice the temperature of the room—and of your own
emotions.
Every word you release either calms or disrupts. Choose
calmness.

You've felt the impact of careless language and seen its quiet
healing when spoken with care.
Composure starts with the breath before speech—the small,
unseen choice to be aware before making sound.

Ask yourself, does what I'm about to say bring us closer to
clarity or push us farther from it?
Let silence guide your wisdom.
Stillness before speaking isn't hesitation; it's true leadership.

Your voice isn't for performance—it's for peace.
When you speak from alignment, your calm becomes
audible.

CHAPTER 8

Boundaries That Protect Belonging

Language Cue: Containment
The discipline of holding space for others without losing yourself in the process.

From Words to What You Hold

Once you learn to regulate what you say, the next challenge is controlling what you hold inside. Communication can stabilize a moment, but containment sustains it. Language may calm the air, but boundaries protect the environment long after the words fade. Without containment, even the most composed voice eventually breaks down under the weight of emotional overflow — yours or others'.

Regulation governs energy within the body: your breath, your tone, your impulse, your inner coherence. It helps you speak clearly in the moment. But containment manages the emotional energy between bodies — the unspoken tension, expectations, urgency, and projection. It influences how much of someone else's experience you permit in and how much of your own you allow out.

Containment is not detachment. It is design.

It is the ability to hold emotional presence without absorbing emotional pressure.

It is choosing what enters your internal world and what must stay outside of it.

It is the structure that protects your clarity, your pace, and your peace.

Where regulation is the pause, containment is the perimeter.

Leaders who regulate without containing become overwhelmed. Leaders who contain without regulating become rigid. But leaders who practice both create environments where calm isn't solely dependent on their endurance — it becomes a shared norm. Their composure acts as a stabilizing force, not a strained performance.

This is where composure shifts from a personal practice to a public safeguard. It becomes part of the relational structure of your leadership — the invisible boundary that allows truth to be spoken without harm, conflict to develop without collapsing, and emotion to surface without taking over the room.

Regulation ensures your words remain steady. Containment guarantees your presence stays safe. Together, they enable you to lead with clarity rather than through crisis, with coherence rather than chaos.

The Paradox of Care

Every great leader starts with care. Care is the instinct that makes you pause, notice, and respond to the humanity in others. However, care without boundaries can quickly turn to chaos. Empathy that flows without limits leads to exhaustion. Compassion without guidance becomes overextension. Support without a structure becomes emotional labor that gradually drains your core.

The paradox of care is that love, service, and belonging all require boundaries. Boundaries are not acts of withdrawing—they are acts of protecting. They make sure that what you give stays generous rather than becoming costly, sustainable rather than sacrificial. People do not feel safest around leaders who give endlessly; they feel safest around leaders who respect the limits of what they can handle. Safety comes not from endless access but from steady self-control.

Boundaries keep the connection clear. They stop emotional leakage—the subtle ways people unconsciously pass along their anxiety, urgency, or fear. They also shield others from absorbing your unspoken resentment or exhaustion. Boundaries ensure that empathy flows smoothly rather than floods, that compassion comforts instead of overwhelms, and that care remains a path rather than a burden.

Containment is the framework that keeps care genuine. It shifts empathy from being open-ended to intentional. It makes clear where your responsibility ends, and someone else's begins. It teaches others how to handle conflict, disappointment, needs, and crisis without falling into you or expecting you to vanish.

The most generous act a composed leader can do is keep a self that remains whole. A leader who stays whole — emotionally, spiritually, and psychologically — fosters a culture where others can do the same. Without structure, generosity turns into self-sacrifice. And without boundaries, connection loses its clarity and becomes confusion.

Care is powerful. But care with containment is transformative. It is the kind of care that sustains rather than drains, guides rather than absorbs, and strengthens rather than scatters. It is leadership that loves without losing itself.

Why Leaders Fear Limits

Many leaders quietly associate boundaries with coldness. They worry that saying no might make them seem unavailable, unkind, or disengaged. As a result, they overextend—taking on extra responsibilities, absorbing others' emotions, and confusing over-functioning with compassion. At first, this may seem like dedication.

Over time, it leads to exhaustion and silent resentment toward the very people they aimed to support. However, resentment is not failure; it is feedback. It indicates where empathy has gone beyond its limits. Boundaries don't diminish generosity—they enhance it. They transform help into well-being. The Mosaic Leader doesn't ask, "How much can I give?" They ask, "How much can I give while remaining whole?" That question shifts care from depletion to sustainability, preventing compassion from collapsing under its own weight.

Containment vs. Control

Boundaries are not walls; they are containers. Control constricts. Containment clarifies. Control says, "Do what I say or chaos will follow." Containment says, "Here's the structure that keeps us safe enough to be honest." When a leader over-controls, people shrink in fear of making mistakes. When they under-contain, people spill—uncertainty and emotion flood the space, eroding trust.

Containment is not only psychological; it is somatic. When leaders define limits clearly, the nervous system interprets that clarity as safety. Boundaries calm cortisol the same way deep breathing does. The composed leader learns to hold the middle ground: firm yet flexible, steady yet responsive. This balance fosters cultures where trust grows naturally. Containment becomes the invisible architecture of emotional safety—the quiet framework that allows creativity to expand within clear boundaries. Boundaries, then, are not rules against relationships; they are the rhythm that makes relationships possible.

The Emotional Cost of Boundary-less Leadership

Without boundaries, leadership turns into emotional babysitting. You start managing everyone's moods instead of guiding the overall direction. You spend more time soothing than strategizing, more time fixing feelings than clarifying priorities. Over time, this imbalance leads to burnout—the silent epidemic among leaders who confuse constant availability with value.

Research from the Center for Creative Leadership (2022) shows that leaders lacking interpersonal boundaries experience 48 percent higher emotional exhaustion and 32 percent lower trust ratings. Boundary strength predicts sustainability more reliably than time management. The Mosaic Way redefines presence: it's not about hours but about quality of attention. You can be completely present for five minutes with clarity and be entirely absent for an hour when fatigued. Composed leaders protect their capacity as deliberately as athletes protect their muscles—through intentional rest and recovery. Because when your energy sinks, your empathy also diminishes. And without empathy, leadership loses its human touch.

Boundaries as Invitations

A boundary isn't a barrier; it's an invitation—a clear statement of mutual respect. When expressed with calm confidence, it tells others, "Here's how we can stay connected without hurting each other." The difference lies entirely in tone and delivery. A defensive boundary feels like rejection; a composed boundary feels like partnership. For example, instead of saying, "Stop interrupting me," you might say, "Let's take turns so we both feel heard." Instead of, "I can't deal with this right now," you could say, "I want to give this the attention it deserves—can we revisit after lunch?" These statements regulate the room while preserving dignity. They protect the connection instead of severing it. A Mosaic Leader uses boundaries not as shields, but as bridges that sustain empathy without erasing self.

Mosaic in Action — The Director Who Redefined Availability

During a high-stakes merger, a nonprofit director found herself absorbing more than just strategy updates. She was absorbing her team's fear. Staff members started sending late-night messages — questions about job security, worries about changing roles, and requests for reassurance. At first, she responded to every message immediately, believing her constant availability would calm the team. It didn't. The more she responded, the more they reached out. Their anxiety increased because they were borrowing her calm.

One night, after answering texts past midnight, she realized she wasn't reassuring anyone — she was rescuing them. And in doing so, she was slowly erasing herself. The next morning, she made a quiet but brave shift. She established a new boundary: any message received after 6 p.m. would be answered the following morning. No exceptions. Then she provided the clarity her team needed: "I'm not becoming less available," she told them in their weekly meeting. "I'm becoming more consistent. You can trust when you'll hear from me, and you can trust that I'll be rested when I respond."

The shift initially felt uncomfortable — for her and for them. But by the second week, something unexpected occurred. The frantic late-night messages decreased. The team started resolving minor problems on their own. People began approaching her during the day instead of spiraling after hours. Within a month, her staff reported feeling calmer and more secure — not because she was available 24/7, but because her availability followed a predictable rhythm.

Her boundary didn't distance the team; it stabilized them. It modeled emotional integrity by honestly naming her limits, cultural flexibility through empathetic communication, and identity agility by choosing a leadership style that reflected who she wanted to be, not who pressure tried to make her. Her limit became a form of leadership—a calming rhythm the team could trust.

By redefining availability, she also redefined safety. And by holding her boundary, she helped everyone, including herself, finally find peace.

Cultural Context and Boundary Expression

Boundaries, like communication, are shaped by culture. In some contexts, directness signals honesty; in others, it feels disrespectful. A composed leader understands that the form of a boundary may change, but its function remains the same: to protect clarity and belonging at the same time. Cultural flexibility ensures that boundaries stay bridges, not barricades. In collectivist cultures, a boundary might be a group norm—"Let's make sure the team rests before deciding." In individualist cultures, it might sound more personal—"I'll need time to process before I respond." In both cases, respect creates containment. Boundaries become universal when they are based not on dominance, but on dignity.

The Language of Limits

When boundaries are new, they often feel unfamiliar and uncomfortable to express. Many leaders hesitate, fearing they might sound rigid, dismissive, or unavailable. But boundaries are simply another way of communicating — and like any language, becoming fluent requires practice, repetition, and intentional use.

The key is balancing warmth with firmness. Boundaries delivered with composure regulate emotions on both sides of the conversation. They preserve dignity while clarifying expectations. This is why composure-based sentence starters matter; they give you structure while your confidence grows.

"To stay clear, here's what I can commit to..."
This phrase centers responsibility without taking on more than is healthy.

"I hear how important this is; let's move it to..."
This communicates empathy while repositioning pace or priority.

"Thank you for sharing this. I'll pause here so I can respond thoughtfully."
This protects your cognitive clarity without shutting down connections.

Each of these phrases performs subtle but powerful work.
They reduce emotional tension. They promote psychological safety.
They indicate that clarity is a sign of care, not rejection.
Over time, this rhythm helps teams to regulate themselves. Emotional overload decreases. Dependency lessens. People learn to self-contain — not by suppressing their needs, but by respecting the structure that allows everyone to function sustainably.

Boundaries teach not only where you end but also where others begin. They encourage shared responsibility rather than resistance. In this way, limits become freeing: they create conditions for trust to deepen, work to flow more smoothly, and relationships to withstand pressure without breaking.

In The Mosaic Way™, this is the leadership language of containment — clarity delivered with compassion. It's a reminder that honoring your limits is not a barrier to connection; it's the foundation that makes meaningful connection possible.

The Self as System

Every leader is more than an individual — you are a living system. Your emotions, beliefs, history, and identity interact similarly to components in any system: they influence each other, reinforce patterns, and shape how you absorb or release pressure. When internal boundaries are weak or unclear, this system becomes porous. Everything gets in. Every request feels urgent. Every critique feels personal. Every challenge seems like a threat.

Internal boundaries establish internal coherence. They help you distinguish what belongs to you from what does not — between your emotional truth and the emotional atmosphere of the room. Without this distinction, leaders carry more than their fair share of emotional weight, often confusing the group's tension with their own failure.

As internal containment develops, you begin to recognize subtle but essential distinctions:

"This feeling is mine,"
— a signal to pause, reflect, and respond with intention.

"That feeling belongs to the group,"
— a reminder that you do not need to absorb collective anxiety to be effective.

"This feedback refines me,"
— an opening for growth.

"That insult doesn't define me,"
— a boundary against unnecessary emotional intrusion.

This clarity does not harden you; it shapes you. It restores your ability to think clearly under pressure and respond without over-identifying. When your internal system stays grounded — its values, its pace, its emotional truth — the external world feels less threatening because it no longer has unchecked access to your inner self.

Calm, then, is not a fixed personality trait or temperament. It is a boundary skill practiced internally—the ability to maintain your center even when others lose theirs. Calm is emotional architecture, an internal framework that stabilizes you before you try to stabilize anyone else.

This is the core of The Mosaic Way™: leadership starts not with controlling the environment but with coherence within oneself. A well-regulated inner system becomes a guiding presence for others.

When the self transforms into a system, and that system becomes coherent, you cease merely reacting to the world and begin engaging with it — grounded, aware, and unmistakably whole.

Micro-Practice — The Three-Breath Boundary Reset

Before re-engaging in a difficult conversation or emotionally charged moment, pause for one minute and practice this sequence:

1. **Breathe:** Name the emotion rising in you.
2. **Bless:** Acknowledge its source without judgment: "This feeling belongs to care, not control."
3. **Bridge:** Choose one action or phrase that honors both care and clarity before re-engaging.
4. This reset prevents empathy from eroding. It re-centers your nervous system so your next word comes from composure, not compulsion.

From Guilt to Grace

High-empathy leaders often feel a surge of guilt when they try to set a boundary. Their instinct is to protect, absorb, and stretch — even when they are already at capacity. They fear that saying no will disappoint others, that pausing will be misunderstood as indifference, or that limiting their availability means limiting their care. This is the burden of the deeply attuned: you feel responsible for everyone's emotional experience, even when it costs you your own.

But boundaries built on guilt are fragile. They fall apart at the first sign of disappointment or pushback. Guilt-based limits sound apologetic, hesitant, and uncertain — a boundary wrapped in a disclaimer. They crumble because they aren't anchored in conviction.

Grace-based boundaries, however, are different. They are compassionate with structure. They sound like:

"I still care, and I also need this to remain sustainable."
"I want to give you my best, and that requires pacing."
"Let's find a way forward that supports both of us."

Grace redefines limits as a form of stewardship — not only for yourself but also for the relationship, the work, and the environment you are shaping. When you communicate with grace, boundaries cease to feel like separation and become a source of support. They serve as a way of tending to the very conditions that make care possible.

Grace-based boundaries recognize a simple truth: you are not withdrawing your presence.

You are protecting your capacity, so your presence remains meaningful.

Over time, guilt begins to dissolve. You no longer feel selfish for protecting your energy; you feel responsible. And others begin to feel safer, not sidelined. They learn that your clarity benefits them — that consistent, honest boundaries create reliability, not distance.

Gradually, guilt turns into gratitude.

You feel thankful for the strength to stay aligned.

They feel thankful for the clarity that guides them on how to engage with you.

That is the quiet miracle of boundaries: once they are respected, everyone breathes more easily. Grace bestows boundaries with dignity — and restores leaders' humanity.

The Mosaic of Containment

Within The Mosaic Way™, containment is a crucial practice that safeguards emotional integrity, transforms cultural flexibility into structure, and provides identity agility with a secure form. It is the choreography of trust — the steady rhythm that keeps the connection graceful rather than chaotic. Without containment, empathy overflows, communication becomes blurry, and even well-intentioned leaders start to lose themselves in the emotional currents of those they serve.

In The Mosaic Advantage™, boundaries form the outer ring of composure—where emotional integrity, cultural flexibility, and identity agility come together. This is where inner awareness turns into external leadership. Boundaries convert personal insight into collective stability. They are not barriers to connection; rather, they are the emotional framework that sustains meaningful interactions.

At their core, boundaries remind us that care and clarity are not rivals but partners in rhythm. Clarity guards care from overextending itself. Care shields clarity from becoming cold. Together, they create a leadership presence that is both strong and gentle, firm and compassionate.

Containment ensures that compassion stays genuine — not twisted by resentment, fatigue, or self-neglect. It allows leadership to remain human, grounded in the reality that no one can give endlessly without boundaries. And it keeps belonging balanced: inclusive without becoming clingy, connected without collapsing into emotional fusion.

A Mosaic Leader doesn't rely on boundaries to control emotions; they use them to choreograph them. Containment directs the flow of connection to prevent anyone — including the leader — from becoming overwhelmed by it. It helps teams feel supported without becoming dependent, and seen without overexposure.

Containment is not suppression; it is stewardship. It involves the disciplined practice of holding emotional space in a way that respects everyone's dignity and capacity. It keeps relationships moving — like dancers moving with purpose — without stepping on each other's toes, losing the rhythm, or disrupting the collective flow.

In this way, containment becomes an act of leadership artistry. It transforms chaos into coherence, empathy into clarity, and connection into a stable, shared rhythm. This is the Mosaic of containment — structure infused with compassion, boundaries shaped by humanity, and leadership guided by grace.

Reflection — Holding Space, Not Weight

Pause and consider:

- Where in my leadership do I confuse care with control?
- Which relationships drain me because my boundaries are unclear?
- How might clarity deepen compassion instead of diminishing it?

Boundaries aren't the end of belonging; they are its container. They prevent empathy from drowning in overextension and keep presence from vanishing under pressure. When you hold space instead of holding weight, you embody the truest form of composure — calm, connected, and capable of sustaining care that endures.

In the next chapter, we'll move from focusing on individual containment to fostering collective care—how entire organizations can establish boundaries that promote trust, equity, and resilience. Because when groups learn to protect belonging together, their composure becomes part of the culture.

!

The Data That Demands Attention

Belonging thrives where clarity exists. In a 2024 McKinsey & Company survey, 62 percent of employees said they struggle to set or respect emotional boundaries at work, leading to rising rates of burnout and role confusion. The Harvard Business School's Leadership and Well-Being Index found that teams with clearly communicated boundaries are 40 percent more productive and report higher psychological safety.

Empathy without limits, data shows, leads to emotional fatigue. A 2023 Gallup workplace report revealed that workers who describe their leaders as "always available" are twice as likely to experience burnout as those whose leaders model balanced accessibility. Healthy containment—knowing when to pause, protect, and redirect—creates the space where care can truly endure.

Boundaries are not barriers; they are foundations for trust. When leaders normalize saying no with grace, they preserve the sense of belonging that honesty maintains. The science of composure confirms what humanity has long understood: love without structure collapses under its own weight.

A Word to the Generations

Generation X
You were rewarded for availability—the open door, the endless day. But leadership now requires discernment. Protecting your time safeguards your integrity.

Millennials
You led the movement toward empathy in management. The next step is sustainable care—learning that compassion with boundaries is what keeps it authentic.

Generation Z
You understand emotional labor instinctively. Protect your empathy intentionally. Boundaries don't isolate you; they enhance your influence.

Generation Alpha
You will grow up in constant communication. Remember that saying "enough for today" isn't rejection—it's self-care. Boundaries will be your quiet superpower.

Generation Beta
You will live in open systems. Boundaries will be how you protect depth, presence, and real connection.

Which part of your generational voice feels strongest right now—clarity, connection, speed, or listening?

The Composed Practice

Composed — Chapter 8:
Boundaries That Protect Belonging

Protection · Clarity · Compassion

I can love deeply and still set boundaries. Boundaries are not
walls—they are wisdom.
I protect my peace to preserve my purpose.

Take a slow breath.
Notice where you've been over-giving.
The tension in your chest isn't resistance—it's recognition.
Your energy is signaling where care has turned into depletion.

Boundaries do not separate; they support. They teach others
how to connect with you, not control you.
Every "no" that honors your integrity is a quiet "yes" to
lasting relationships.

Place your hand over your heart and whisper, "My peace is
my responsibility." Let that truth settle like an anchor in
the ocean of expectation.

You do not lose a sense of belonging when you set
boundaries—you redefine it.
Real belonging only exists where respect and restoration
meet.

CHAPTER 9 ————————————————

Restoring Rhythm: Why Composure Is a Practice, Not a Performance

Language Cue: Renewal
The rhythm of returning — to center, to presence, to yourself.

The Illusion of Arriving

L eaders love finish lines. We crave that moment of arrival that promises we've finally "made it"—that the stress, struggle, and endless self-correction have brought us to some lasting state of ease. Yet composure doesn't work that way. There is no final calm, only practiced recovery. There is no fixed balance, only ongoing realignment. The myth of arrival convinces us to perform steadiness rather than cultivate it—to look composed instead of becoming composed.

Real composure isn't flawless; it's fluid. It bends, breathes, and begins again. The composed leader doesn't aim to stay perfectly balanced; they learn to notice when the rhythm shifts. They hear the subtle cues—the tightening jaw, the rising pace, the shallower breath—that signal misalignment. And instead of collapsing in shame, they restore rhythm with awareness. That act of return isn't weakness; it's wisdom—the quiet mastery of a leader who understands that calm isn't something you keep; it's something you continually return to.

Performance vs. Practice

Performance seeks approval; practice seeks alignment. Performance says, "If I appear calm, people will trust me." Practice says, "If I stay grounded, people will feel safe with me." Performance hides fatigue and suppresses emotion; practice honors both as data points in the leadership process. One builds an image; the other builds integrity.

Composure exhibited is fragile—it fractures under scrutiny because it's based on control. Composure cultivated is resilient—it adapts itself mid-movement because it's rooted in awareness. The Mosaic Way™ teaches that composure is not a mask to hold but a rhythm to maintain connection. It's a daily return to honesty with oneself, a dedication to alignment that surpasses perfection. A leader grounded in practice understands that presence is not about being unshakable; it's about being able to recover.

The Sound of Disconnection

Disconnection always reveals itself—not through words, but through tone. You notice it in the sharpness of your speech, sense it in the impatience of your breath, and see it in the fatigue shadowing your compassion. You begin reacting more quickly and recovering more slowly. A low hum of unease starts to influence your decisions—a quiet feeling that your pace no longer aligns with your purpose.

That hum is not failure; it's feedback. It's your inner metronome whispering, "You're offbeat. Return to tempo." Ignoring it leads to depletion; listening to it leads to renewal. Restoration begins with noticing—when your thoughts race ahead of your values, when your empathy lags behind your actions, when your leadership becomes mechanical instead of mindful. Awareness is the first act of composure. It interrupts performance and opens the door to recovery.

Micro-Practices of Recalibration

Composure isn't rebuilt through grand retreats or long breaks. It's restored through small, everyday acts of being present. You don't need hours of silence to reset; you need quick moments of awareness scattered throughout the day—tiny practices that bring you back into sync before chaos takes over.

When your rhythm begins to slip, pause before responding and take a few seconds to breathe before every emotionally charged reply. This simple action rewires reactivity into regulation. Silently acknowledge what's real: My chest is tight. My pulse is fast. Awareness stabilizes physiology before emotion can escalate. Recenter physically—plant both feet, straighten your posture, and exhale completely; grounding the body re-anchors the mind. Then, reassess your stance by asking, Am I acting from fear or integrity? The answer guides your next move. Finally, make quick repairs. When tone or timing breaks the connection, identify it and reset; each repair strengthens emotional maturity.

Small disciplines, practiced regularly, develop the muscle memory of calm. Over time, these quiet rituals become second nature—a rhythm you can return to regardless of how chaotic the surroundings are.

The Recovery Loop

Every leader experiences the same cyclical process: regulation, disruption, and repair.

This cycle is universal. It represents the emotional choreography of being human — and of being responsible for others. The speed, gentleness, and intentionality with which you navigate this cycle define your true resilience.

Regulation is the steadiness you develop — the breath you take before responding, the tone you choose when under stress, the awareness that keeps your presence grounded.

Disruption occurs when fatigue, pressure, conflict, or emotion disturbs that steadiness.

Disruption is not a sign of weakness; it is a natural outcome of engaging deeply with the world.

Repair is the deliberate act of returning — the choice to realign without shame, to restore your tone, your clarity, and your connection.

Many leaders misunderstand disruption as failure. They think that losing composure equals losing credibility. However, disruption is not only unavoidable — it shows that you are alive, engaged, and emotionally committed. Leaders who never disrupt are often not fully present.

The goal is not to avoid disruption but to recover more quickly and intentionally. Recovery is resilience in action. It is the skill that transforms emotional intelligence from a concept into action. When you learn to move smoothly through this process, your leadership becomes rhythmic instead of reactive. You stop just performing calm and start truly embodying it.

And something remarkable happens: you transform composure from a personal virtue into a shared rhythm.

Your team is beginning to mirror your recovery pace. Your willingness to repair encourages others to do the same. Trust deepens not because you never wobble, but because you don't hide it — and you know how to return with grace.

This is what establishes credibility in the modern workplace: Not perfection, not emotional stillness, but the visible, honest practice of repair.

Each time you restore your rhythm, you demonstrate emotional maturity. Each time you recover from a disruption, you help stabilize the room. Each time you repair, you invite others to realign with themselves.

The Recovery Loop becomes a culture-shaping pattern—a collective breathing rhythm. It shifts leadership from pressure to presence and from performance to coherence.

The Rhythm of Teams

A team's tempo often reflects its leader's nervous system. When a leader loses rhythm, the group feels it; when that leader regains rhythm, the group learns it. Composure spreads through teams via subtle mechanisms of mirroring and attunement. When you speak calmly, others' nervous systems align with your steadiness. When you pause before reacting, you foster reflection rather than reactivity.

Over time, your team internalizes this rhythm. Meetings slow just enough for meaning to surface. Disagreements develop into dialogue. Energy that was once scattered in stress refocuses into shared purpose. This is how emotional culture transforms—not through policies or slogans, but through leaders who embody regulation. The Mosaic Advantage™ was never meant to exist in isolation; it was designed to ripple outward, turning individual composure into collective calm.

Rest as Strategy

In a world obsessed with urgency and constant visibility, rest has become an act of rebellion. Modern systems reward exhaustion and mistake stillness for weakness. Yet every rhythm—musical, emotional, or organizational—needs pauses to stay harmonious. Rest isn't the opposite of productivity; it's the renewal of perspective.

Without rest, empathy diminishes, creativity falters, and composure becomes a rehearsed act—a hollow display of calm. The composed leader considers rest an essential part of the work. They allocate time for recovery as they do for meetings, recognizing that silence is where meaning is renewed. Rest is not indulgence; it is the foundation. Without it, the structure of leadership begins to break down.

Repairing with Grace

Composure weakens most when pride blocks repair. Leaders fear that admitting a mistake might weaken authority, so they try to control more. But repair isn't weakness; it's wisdom. Saying, "I overreacted earlier; let's reset," shows maturity, not failure. Admitting, "That meeting threw me off balance," shows honesty, not instability.

Grace heals faster than guilt because it encourages connection rather than shame. It reminds everyone that leadership is a human rhythm, not a mechanical act. The Mosaic Way™ teaches that composure isn't about never losing rhythm; it's about learning how to rejoin the music without disrupting the song. Each time you repair with grace, you strengthen a culture where honesty and humility coexist.

Returning to Stillness

Stillness is not stagnation; it's structure—the anchor that gives motion meaning. Returning to stillness, whether mentally, emotionally, or spiritually, allows you to reclaim authorship of your own tempo. It is the quiet pause between beats, the breath between decisions, the subtle reminder that you are not defined by pace but by presence.

You don't find stillness by escaping movement but by aligning within it. When what you feel, believe, and do are in harmony, peace emerges—not as a luxury, but as a natural outcome. Stillness is where coherence becomes visible. It doesn't remove you from leadership; it restores the humanity that sustains leadership.

The Mosaic of Renewal

Emotional integrity keeps you honest. Cultural flexibility keeps you connected. Identity agility keeps you evolving. Together, these skills create the rhythm of composure—steady enough to support others, flexible enough to adapt, strong enough to renew through disruption. You are not meant to perform calm; you are meant to embody it. The Mosaic Way™ has never been about perfection; it has always been about wholeness.

So when your rhythm stumbles, don't hide. Return. Return to your breath. Return to your truth. Return to the person behind the performance. Leadership isn't about keeping a steady tempo; it's about restoring harmony when the world falls out of tune.

Reflection — The Practice of Becoming

Pause for renewal and ask yourself:

- What does calm look like when I'm no longer trying to prove it?
- Where in my day do I need recovery — not as a reward, but as a rhythm?
- How can I portray restoration so others realize they don't need to maintain composure to belong?

Composure isn't what you hold; it's what holds you. It's the rhythm you return to when the world shakes — the melody that stays even when the song changes. Keep returning. Keep breathing. Keep becoming. That is the Mosaic Advantage™ — not perfection achieved, but presence practiced.

!

The Data That Demands Attention

Recovery is now recognized as a vital performance factor. The American Institute of Stress reported in 2024 that 77 percent of professionals regularly experience physical or emotional exhaustion due to high-pressure work environments. However, fewer than 30 percent of leaders intentionally include recovery practices in their routines.

Neuroscience confirms what intuition has long known: the brain's prefrontal cortex—responsible for judgment, empathy, and complex decision-making—needs cycles of rest to maintain clarity. Research from Stanford University shows that leaders who keep consistent sleep and recovery patterns have 40 percent higher cognitive adaptability and are less likely to make reactive decisions. The data show that composure is biological as much as behavioral; restoration supports regulation.

Organizations that promote rest culture see measurable benefits. The 2024 Deloitte Global Resilience Index showed that teams encouraged to take breaks between projects have 35 percent higher retention and significantly better innovation scores. Calm, it turns out, is not passive—it's preparatory.

A Word to the Generations

 **Generation X**
You equated worth with endurance. But the new measure of mastery is rhythm—knowing when to engage and when to exhale. Rest is leadership in motion.

 **Millennials**
You've spent years balancing ambition and exhaustion. Let recovery become part of your definition of success. You lead most effectively when your energy speaks before your fatigue does.

 **Generation Z**
You are redefining work-life balance with courage. Protect your quiet spaces; they are not escapes from growth but opportunities to sustain it.

 **Generation Alpha**
You will inherit an always-on world. Learn early that slowing down is not losing pace — it's preserving purpose. Rhythm will keep your brilliance steady.

 **Generation Beta**
You will be taught to optimize time. Rhythm will teach you when to rest, return, and begin again.

Which part of your generational voice feels strongest right now—clarity, connection, speed, or listening?

The Composed Practice

Composed — Chapter 9: Restoring Rhythm

Recovery · Renewal · Flow

I am permitted to pause. Stillness isn't failure; it's feedback.
I return to rhythm, not perfection.

Breathe.
Feel the pulse beneath your hand — steady, patient,
    unhurried.
This is the sound of composure returning home.

Pressure teaches urgency, but wisdom guides pace.
When you slow down, clarity catches up.
When you rest, what matters most surfaces.

Ask yourself, where have I been rushing through what needs
    rhythm?
Notice how often performance has taken the place of
    presence.
Then, let go of the need to keep up and start again — slower,
    truer.

Your rhythm is your resilience. You don't earn calm; you
    practice it.
And each time you return, you become more whole.

PART IV _____

The Path Home

Language Cue: Belonging
The return to self after seasons of holding everything together.

The Quiet Threshold

There comes a point in every journey when the effort quiets down. The titles that once defined you, the strategies that once protected you, the composure you've spent so much time maintaining — all begin to loosen their hold. What takes their place isn't less ambition but more honesty. Not less movement but more purpose. The Path Home starts in that space — when leadership stops being about proving oneself and begins about returning.

By now, you have built an architecture of alignment: emotional integrity anchoring your truth, cultural flexibility expanding your empathy, and identity agility allowing you to evolve without losing yourself. You've learned the rhythm of recovery, the discipline of boundaries, and the language of calm. And now, this final section asks you to do what few leaders ever dare — to come home to yourself. Not the version of you shaped by expectation, nor the one polished by performance, but the one who leads because they are finally whole.

After the Fire

Pressure changes everything. For some, it refines; for others, it reveals. But for most, it burns away what no longer belongs. If you've experienced enough upheaval—personally, professionally, or both—you already understand that composure can't be learned from theory. It is gained through repair. It is born in moments when you break under the weight you never expected to bear, in conversations that shatter the illusion of control, and in the fatigue that whispers, You can't keep leading like this.

This stage of the journey is not about performance — it's about healing. Pressure always leaves a mark, but that mark can become wisdom if you choose to tend to it instead of hiding it. Every leader bears fractures — invisible seams that tell the story of survival. The Mosaic Way does not erase those cracks; it arranges them into strength. Like light passing through stained glass, your fractures become the very channels through which wisdom shines.

Wholeness as Return

For generations, leadership models have focused outward—toward growth, innovation, and progress. But wisdom eventually turns inward and asks, What good is growth if it outpaces your soul? Wholeness isn't just moving forward; it's a circular journey—a return to center after seasons of stretch. You don't find peace by running faster. You find it by realizing you were never meant to run alone.

The path home is not a retreat from ambition but a return to alignment — that rare moment when purpose and presence finally share the same space. When your outer leadership mirrors your inner life, calm stops being just a skill and becomes a way of being. You cease chasing stability and start embodying it. Wholeness isn't the absence of pursuit; it's the presence of coherence — a life where meaning moves in sync with momentum. This is what it means to lead without losing yourself.

Repair as Reentry

In these closing chapters, we'll explore how composure grows through repair — how to reconnect what pressure fractured, how to turn Mosaic awareness into everyday actions, and how to move forward without breaking apart again. Repair isn't about restoring things to how they once were; it's about rebuilding them stronger, softer, and truer. It means shifting from performance to presence, from reaction to rhythm, from exhaustion to renewal.

Homecoming requires humility—the courage to acknowledge that I am still learning how to be whole while I lead. That statement is not a sign of weakness; it reflects wisdom. It admits that mastery is not the absence of struggle but the integration of learning. The final stage of composure is not control—it is self-trust renewed through grace. It is the moment when leadership shifts from managing others to reconciling yourself.

The Mosaic of Return

Throughout this book, the Mosaic has symbolized integration — the process of uniting shattered pieces into wholeness. But as you stand at this final threshold, it transforms into something more: a compass. Each tile now signifies a truth you've lived, a value you've reclaimed, a lesson you've learned. They fit together differently than before — not because you've lost pieces, but because you've grown around them. The image has shifted, but the core remains.

The path home is not about recreating who you were before disruption; it is about integrating who you have become because of it. When you can see your evolution without judgment — when you can honor both the strength and the scar — you've arrived at wholeness. The Mosaic is no longer a framework to follow; it's a reflection of you. The journey has not made you flawless. It has made you real.

Reflection — Coming Home to Yourself

Pause here before stepping into the final chapters and ask yourself:

- What has pressure taught me that peace never could?
- Which parts of me fractured under leadership, and which have quietly healed?
- What does home really feel like — not just as a place, but as a presence?

The path home isn't straight; it's a journey. It's the gentle process of remembering, realigning, and resting in the truth that composure was never about holding everything together — it was about learning how to hold yourself. And when you do, the mosaic doesn't just shine — it radiates, not from perfection, but from peace.

CHAPTER 10 ———————————

Repairing What Pressure Broke

Language Cue: Restoration
The art of rebuilding connection — with yourself, your people, and your purpose — after the fracture of pressure.

From Rhythm to Repair

W hen rhythm returns, repair becomes the next crucial step. Composure reestablishes your connection with yourself—your breath, your clarity, your internal tempo. However, repair addresses the pressure that may have disturbed you. Rhythm restores the individual; repair mends the relationship. It is the moment when your steadiness begins to extend beyond your body and into the shared space with others.

Repair is the sound of recovery—the music that rises after the silence of strain. It signals that emotional turbulence has passed, that safety is returning, and that connection can be rebuilt with intention rather than urgency. While renewal helps you stand upright again, restoration asks how you will move forward from that grounded place. Rhythm puts you back in alignment; repair invites others back into alignment with you.

This is where composure develops into leadership that heals. Repair turns calm from a private state into a public offering—one that rebuilds trust without rushing forgiveness, clarifies expectations without assigning blame, and restores dignity without ignoring what happened. In this phase, your presence becomes a stabilizing force. People sense that the conflict, pressure, or rupture did not pull you off your center, and that steadiness becomes the bridge back to relational coherence.

Repair isn't about pretending nothing happened. It's about creating the conditions for honesty, accountability, and reconnection. It is the leadership work that transforms emotional regulation into relational renewal—where your internal rhythm sets the pace for collective healing and restores a sense of belonging.

The Quiet After the Breaking

There's always a moment after pressure when the noise quiets down. The meeting ends, adrenaline dips, and what's left isn't relief—it's residue. The tension that once fueled performance lingers in your shoulders. The words you didn't intend to say echo in your mind. The relationships you strained sit heavy in the silence. Every leader knows this moment—the quiet after the storm—when composure feels fake and self-trust feels far away.

Yet, repair begins exactly there — not when everything is fixed but when you stop pretending it isn't broken. Pressure doesn't just test systems; it tests souls. And what it cracks most often isn't competence but connection: belonging to yourself, your team, and your truth. What you do in that quiet moment determines whether the fracture becomes a scar or a source of strength.

Pressure and the Myth of Strength

We are conditioned to judge leadership by endurance—by who can carry the most weight, stay calm the longest, and sacrifice the deepest without showing strain. But relentless strength ultimately isolates. The more you maintain control, the less approachable you become. The more you hide tiredness, the more fragile your empathy becomes. Pressure leads you to believe that composure equals suppression—that to command the room, you must hold your breath.

Composure isn't about not feeling at all; it's about feeling fully and still functioning. Healing begins when you stop hiding behind resilience and start honoring your humanity. Pressure doesn't always create diamonds. Sometimes, it cracks foundations—and that's okay. Cracks aren't failures; they are pathways for light to return. The Mosaic Way™ teaches that light through fracture is still illumination—perhaps the most genuine kind.

Emotional Debris

Every period of high pressure leaves behind emotional debris— fragments of guilt, unspoken tension, and the quiet dissonance between who you intended to be and how you actually showed up. Most leaders rush past this stage, eager to reclaim normalcy. But unprocessed emotion doesn't dissolve; it deposits. It settles into the body as defensiveness, restlessness, or distance.

Repairing lives happens both in reflection and in the body. The shoulders that once held tension must learn to let go; the breath that shortened under stress must expand again. Physical release completes emotional healing. The calm leader doesn't rush to move forward; they pause to look inward. They ask themselves: What part of me was under pressure and needed protection? What truth did I hide to keep my composure? What relationship or rhythm now calls for repair? Awareness clears the emotional debris before it turns into disconnection.

Repairing Trust with Yourself

The toughest repair is the one no one notices—the quiet effort of rebuilding trust with yourself. You recall the moments you lost your temper, the conversations you dodged, the decisions driven by fear rather than honesty. Self-trust doesn't shatter loudly; it breaks in silence, but its absence influences everything.

Repair starts not with punishment but with honesty. Shame says, 'You failed.' Integrity says, 'You faltered—now learn.' When you tell yourself the truth without judgment, you reopen the channel of compassion that pressure had closed. Self-compassion is not indulgence; it is the foundation. You can't extend grace to others while withholding it from yourself. What you say to yourself in private reflects the tone others hear in public.

Reconnecting with Others

Pressure distorts communication long before it ruins the connection. Words become sharper, empathy grows thinner, and listening fades away. The Mosaic Way™ teaches that repairing relationships starts not with explanation but with acknowledgment. People don't need your reasons first; they need your recognition.

Start with impact: "I know my tone in that meeting created distance." Own your contribution: "That wasn't aligned with how I want to lead." Then invite collaboration: "Can we talk about what would rebuild trust for you?" Repair is not rebranding; it is reconciliation—a rhythm of awareness rather than a single act of apology. When you own rupture without defensiveness, you model the very safety others need to do the same. That is how trust begins to breathe again.

Mosaic in Action — The Manager Who Rebuilt Trust

After a tense product-launch meeting, a department manager walked back to her office feeling a heaviness she couldn't shake. Under pressure, she had dismissed her team's concerns, pushed past their hesitation, and rushed toward a deadline with a sharper tone than she intended. No one confronted her, but she noticed the subtle signals — quiet cameras during the debrief, shorter responses in chat, and a noticeable drop in the creative energy her team usually brought. She realized she hadn't just shut down a discussion; she had shut down a connection.

The next morning, she chose repair over avoidance. Instead of pretending nothing happened, she called a ten-minute reset session and acknowledged the situation plainly: "Yesterday, I dismissed valid concerns because I was stressed. That's not the leader I want to be.

I'm here to repair it." Her honesty softened the room. Then she asked a simple but powerful question: "What would help you feel fully heard again?" One by one, team members shared their needs — clarity in timelines, space to disagree, and reassurance that raising risks would be seen as contribution, not resistance.

Her willingness to repair shifted everything. Over the next few weeks, engagement increased. Decision-making became more collaborative. Team members offered ideas before she asked. The initiative was returned not because she demanded it, but because psychological safety was restored. The manager's composure didn't just steady herself; it realigned the group. The team rediscovered its rhythm as she rediscovered her own.

Her repair showcased the Mosaic Advantage™ — emotional honesty in acknowledging the rupture, cultural adaptability in listening across power and perspective differences, and identity agility in adjusting her leadership without defensiveness. By choosing restoration over perfection, she rebuilt trust and reignited momentum. The team moved forward because she turned composure into connection.

When Systems Fracture

Not every break is emotional. Some are structural: broken communication loops, overwhelmed teams, cultures that reward burnout more than balance. Pressure exposes fault lines already hidden beneath the surface. The work of repair, then, is not just restoration—it is redesign.

A composed leader doesn't merely patch cracks; they reimagine the foundation. They ask, What system failed under stress? What value was lost in the rush? What rhythm needs protection next time? Organizational repair requires maturity—the willingness to confront dysfunction without denial and to design differently rather than defend what was.

This is where Performance with Presence™ truly shows its value: redesigning systems that maintain composure under pressure instead of relying on individuals to bear that burden. At this level, composure becomes a matter of collective integrity in action—a shared understanding that mistakes are opportunities to improve, not reasons to withdraw.

Forgiveness as Leadership

Forgiveness is one of leadership's most misunderstood strengths. It is not a sign of weakness; it is a sign of wisdom. Forgiveness doesn't eliminate accountability—it frees you from clinging to the version of events that keeps you stuck. It opens up space for new actions, new conversations, and new possibilities.

Forgiving yourself restores internal rhythm; forgiving others restores relational rhythm. Both reclaim the emotional energy you need for the future. Forgiveness doesn't mean forgetting — it means leading from the lesson rather than the wound. Leaders who forgive quietly and genuinely rebuild faster because they waste less energy defending pain. They convert that energy into peace, creating emotional oxygen for everyone around them. Forgiveness, then, is not just a moral virtue; it's strategic restoration.

Restoring Emotional Rhythm

Emotional rhythm is the flow between action and reflection, between giving and receiving, between leading and listening. Pressure disrupts that flow; repair restores it. You rebuild rhythm by reintroducing deliberate cycles—pausing before reacting, reflecting before deciding, recovering before returning.

Modern leadership often values continuous results, but recovery needs effort: time, reflection, and renewal. Insight must replenish what performance has exhausted. A composed leader makes space for that renewal, understanding that stillness is not laziness but strategy. Over time, this rhythm becomes familiar— the steady pulse of the Mosaic Leader™: measured, grounded, responsive, whole.

Repair as Collective Practice

When practiced effectively, repair becomes part of the culture. Healthy organizations embrace imperfection and promote recovery. They substitute fear-driven accountability with dialogue-centered learning. In a Mosaic culture, repair resembles curiosity rather than blame: What went wrong and why? What can we learn instead of asking who to blame? How can we design systems that withstand stress better next time?

Repair rituals build psychological safety—the emotional foundation that supports growth without ongoing harm. They serve as reminders that mistakes are not disqualifying; avoidance is. When teams repair together, they become more resilient as a unit. When repair becomes a shared language, trust becomes a collective reflex rather than an individual achievement.

Grace as the Final Strength

Every path through composure leads here—to grace. Grace is not softness; it is the stamina of the spirit, the quiet power to remain kind after disappointment, hopeful after disruption, human after humiliation. Pressure breaks everyone differently: some lose trust, others lose confidence, and still others lose faith. Grace rebuilds all three.

Grace is what wisdom sounds like after surviving. It is the deep knowing that effort is never wasted, even if reconciliation never happens. Every attempt to heal makes you stronger, softer, and more complete. Grace doesn't erase the fracture; it redefines it. It turns what was once painful into a pathway for empathy—the purest sign of evolved leadership.

The Mosaic of Repair

Repair is the ongoing practice that keeps the Mosaic alive. It transforms leadership fractures into signs of wisdom. Emotional Integrity helps you reveal the truth about what has cracked. Cultural Flexibility enables you to reconnect across differences. Identity

Agility helps you integrate who you were under pressure with who you are becoming now.

Together, these capacities transform brokenness into design. Composure isn't maintained by perfection; it's renewed through repair. Every restoration reminds us that leadership isn't about remaining unbroken—it's about becoming whole again, each time differently. Repair is the final rhythm of composure and the first note of culture—the bridge between your individual calm and the collective peace you foster.

Reflection — Rebuilding from the Inside Out

Pause here and reflect:

- Which aspect of my leadership still requires reconciliation?
- Whose trust have I regained — and whose have I subtly avoided confronting?
- What system, inside or around me, needs to be redesigned to prevent the same fracture?

Repair is not the end of composure; it is its renewal. Because everything that broke under pressure can be restored with grace. You don't have to be flawless to be trusted. You only need to be willing to rebuild — again and again, until restoration becomes your rhythm.

!

The Data That Demands Attention

Repair is a tangible skill, not just a sentimental act. In a 2024 MIT Sloan Management Review study, 72 percent of employees said that how a leader responds after conflict influences their long-term trust more than the conflict itself. The Gottman Institute's research on relational dynamics echoes this idea: relationships—whether personal or professional—succeed not by avoiding rupture, but by practicing timely repair.

The cost of neglect is high. A 2023 Gallup survey found that teams that fail to address emotional fractures experience 37 percent lower engagement and significantly slower recovery from organizational stress. By contrast, when leaders openly admit mistakes, take responsibility, and rebuild trust, psychological safety quickly recovers, and cooperation improves.

Pressure naturally tests human systems; what defines sustainable leadership is not perfection but the ability to repair. The data shows that maintaining composure without reconciliation causes distance, while maintaining composure with empathy helps rebuild the foundation of trust.

A Word to the Generations

 You were taught to move on quickly—to fix problems, not to feel. But healing needs presence, not just action. Courage now means going back to the room you left too soon.

 You value transparency but often feel guilty about emotional wounds. Remember: repair doesn't erase failure; it turns it into growth. Apology is a sign of advanced leadership.

 You expect authenticity and accountability from those in power. Maintain that standard, but lead by example. The grace you show will shape your influence just as much as the truth you speak.

 You will grow up in a world that records every mistake. Learn early that fixing errors is more important than reputation. The essence of leadership is how you recover after a rupture.

 You will witness systems fail in public. Repair will be your quiet leadership—choosing restoration over replacement.

Which part of your generational voice feels strongest right now—clarity, connection, speed, or listening?

The Composed Practice

Composed — Chapter 10: Repairing What Pressure Broke

Restoration · Grace · Reconnection

I can start again without shame.
Repair is not weakness; it's wisdom.
What broke under pressure can be rebuilt with grace.

Take a breath that touches the parts of you still holding guilt.
Let it soften what perfection once hardened. You don't need
to perform forgiveness; you only need to accept it.

Every leader breaks under pressure. What matters is how
you recover. Repair starts with honesty, grows through
empathy, and ends with understanding.
You are not defined by the moment you broke — but by the
moment you chose to heal.

Ask yourself, *What deserves repair, not resentment?*
Who needs to see that I can be both accountable and kind?

Whisper softly, I am still deserving of trust—even from
myself.
Let that truth bridge the gap between who you were and who
you are becoming.

CHAPTER 11 ——————————————

The Mosaic Advantage

Language Cue: Integration
The convergence of language, emotion, and identity into authentic, sustainable leadership.

From Repair to Integration

Every cycle of composure ends the same way — not in perfection, but in integration. Repair helps you rebuild what pressure strain, but integration teaches you how to live inside that rebuilt space without bracing for the next impact. It is the moment when healing shifts from an event to a lifestyle, when you stop treating composure as something you only access in crisis and start to move with it in everyday life.

After repair, what remains is rhythm. After rhythm, what remains is truth. Repair restores connection; rhythm restores coherence; integration restores identity. It is the phase where the lessons of recovery settle into your body and start shaping how you speak, decide, and lead. Chapter 10 showed you how to mend the fractures caused by pressure. This chapter asks a deeper question: What happens when the repair is complete, and you are no longer leading from urgency but from understanding?

Integration is where recovery becomes coherence—where the pieces of you that once felt scattered begin to move as one. It is the space where emotional integrity, cultural flexibility, and identity agility work together rather than compete for attention. You stop performing calm and start embodying it. You stop managing strain and begin designing your life around what keeps you grounded. Leadership stops reaching for balance and starts becoming it.

This is the quiet maturity of composure: the point where steadiness is no longer something you struggle to maintain but something you naturally fall back into. Integration does not guarantee the end of pressure; it guarantees that pressure will no longer break you down. It turns composure into a rhythm you can trust—one that invites others into stability just by being present.

The Integration Point

Every leader hits a point when their techniques stop working. The affirmations, frameworks, and carefully rehearsed strategies — all start to feel like armor that no longer fits. The only question that remains is: Who am I when the tools are gone?

The Mosaic Advantage™ starts with integration, not more tactics. When your emotional integrity, cultural flexibility, and identity agility work together as one rhythm, a fundamental shift occurs. You stop leading from reaction and begin leading from coherence. Integration isn't just an achievement; it's an alignment—when your words, values, and presence stop competing and start harmonizing.

In that harmony, leadership feels less like control and more like a composition — an orchestration of steadiness expressed through language, tone, and intentional action. It's no longer about managing perception; it's about moving with authenticity. This is the moment when the leader stops performing and starts embodying.

The Power of Wholeness

Wholeness isn't about being fixed; it's about being fluent in your own humanity. Fragmented leaders chase perfection, constantly managing their appearance instead of their true selves. Integrated leaders understand that people follow congruence, not charisma —

truth, not performance. They attract those whose presence feels like alignment.

You can't fake coherence. When your inner state conflicts with your outer message, people notice it immediately. But when your words, tone, and energy align, trust flows easily. The Mosaic Advantage™ is in that felt safety — when you're calm, it encourages others to stop performing and be authentic. Your genuine nature empowers them to be themselves.

Integration starts with awareness but manifests in embodiment. When your breath steadies before your words form, and your shoulders relax as your tone softens, coherence shifts from a concept to a physical authority.

The Language of Integration

Language is the outward reflection of inner coherence. Every word you speak either enhances alignment or reveals fragmentation. The confident leader doesn't chase perfect phrasing; they speak from an anchored center. Clarity doesn't come from memorized scripts — it flows from consistent values.

Three Mosaic language shifts guide this integration: move from performance to presence ("I have to prove this" becomes "I want to contribute this"), from command to collaboration ("You need to fix this" becomes "Let's rebuild this"), and from certainty to curiosity ("Here's the right way" becomes "Here's what I'm noticing").

These shifts may seem subtle, but they indicate deep maturity. They show that your leadership is based on confidence in shared ability rather than fear of losing control. Words that regulate, relate, and reveal are the language of the composed. When aligned with integrity, language becomes the foundation of trust.

Emotional Literacy as Strength

Emotional literacy — the ability to recognize, name, and manage emotion — has become a central form of intelligence in contemporary leadership. It is not just a soft skill; it is strategic clarity.

When you can identify your internal state, you avoid getting caught in storms. You notice frustration building before it affects your tone. You sense anxiety in others before it turns into resistance.

This literacy enables you to regulate emotions without repression and empathize without losing yourself. The Mosaic Leader doesn't just manage emotion; they interpret it. They recognize that behind every reaction is a need, and behind each need is a story. Emotional literacy turns reactive energy into relational intelligence.

This fluency gives you an edge no system can replicate. While technology can optimize, only humans can empathize. The emotionally intelligent leader navigates uncertainty with grounded presence — the rare ability to stay both aware and available when others withdraw.

Identity Agility — Leading as a Whole Self

Identity agility is the ability to adapt your leadership without losing yourself. Rigid leaders fail when circumstances change because their sense of self is tied to their role rather than to their purpose. Agile leaders grow because they realize that leadership is something they embody, not something they defend.

When your sense of self is secure, you can shift seamlessly between roles — mentor and learner, director and listener, strategist and servant — without losing coherence. You can change form without losing your core. This flexibility keeps you human within systems that demand speed and reinvention.

Identity agility isn't about shapeshifting to please others; it's about expanding to meet the moment. It's the skill of staying consistent in your values while being adaptable in how you express them — to remain "you" even as "you" evolve. That's the mark of maturity in motion.

Cultural Flexibility — Leadership as Translation

In an interconnected world, culture isn't just background — it's bandwidth. Cultural flexibility means being able to navigate differences without losing connection. The composed leader doesn't see diversity as a complication but as communication — an ongoing conversation about meaning.

Culturally flexible leaders listen to understand others' intent, not just their words. They bridge perspectives without losing meaning or clarity. This isn't about political correctness; it's about emotional correctness — respecting the human context in every interaction.

When you model cultural flexibility, you shift belonging from conformity to curiosity. You turn diversity from tension into innovation. The Mosaic Leader becomes a bridge—a translator of values across boundaries, creating environments where empathy grows, and misunderstanding diminishes.

The Architecture of The Mosaic Advantage™

The Mosaic Advantage™ is based on a layered structure—three concentric capacities that reinforce each other from the inside out. At the core is **Emotional Integrity**, the inner layer where self-awareness stabilizes, and truth becomes your anchor. This forms the foundation of composed leadership: the ability to identify what you feel, honor what you value, and manage what you express. Without emotional integrity, every other skill is just performance. With it, presence becomes credible because it is grounded in honesty rather than image.

Surrounding the center is **Cultural Flexibility**, the middle layer where connection broadens. Here, leaders master the art of meeting people where they are without abandoning their own stance. Cultural flexibility is not about assimilation; it's about attunement — the ability to honor differences with dignity, translate across perspectives, and navigate tension without shrinking or dominating. When emotional integrity provides clarity, cultural flexibility extends your reach. It enables your leadership to cross cultures, personalities, and contexts while remaining coherent.

The outermost layer is **Identity Agility**, the broad ring that maintains adaptability. This layer shows the leader's ability to develop without losing themselves, to change roles and rhythms while staying anchored internally. Identity agility makes you responsive without being reactive, innovative without losing your footing. It is the skill that helps leaders grow with their environments rather than fall apart under them.

Together, these three layers create the integrated leader — clear internally, connected externally, and consistent throughout. The Mosaic Advantage™ is more than a model; it's a guiding principle. It transforms self-awareness into strategy, empathy into influence, and presence into a stabilizing force. When all three abilities work together in harmony, leadership shifts from merely managing pressure to transforming it. Integration becomes the process through which leaders heal rather than hurt, connect rather than disconnect, and influence with integrity rather than force.

This is the architecture that makes composed leadership possible. It's not about perfection but about practice — the continuous process of aligning what you feel, how you relate, and who you are becoming.

The Mosaic in Motion

When emotional integrity, cultural flexibility, and identity agility align, something transformative occurs: the leader begins to dissolve, and presence takes over. Leadership is no longer driven by effort, image, or control — it flows through coherence. Composure becomes more than just steadiness; it becomes movement. Influence becomes an invitation rather than an imposition. Leadership evolves into authentic alignment, where who you are and how you lead become indistinguishable.

You'll recognize the Mosaic in motion through subtle shifts rather than dramatic moments. Meetings end with clarity, not exhaustion. Difficult conversations settle instead of spiraling. People leave your presence more grounded than when they arrived. Your team begins to regulate themselves through the rhythm you embody. Urgency stops dictating the emotional climate. Energy in the room no longer spikes and crashes; it flows — steady, intentional, responsive. These are the quiet signatures of composure practiced consistently.

The Mosaic Way™ isn't a manual to memorize; it's a rhythm to embody. It teaches you how to navigate complexity without losing your internal compass and to adapt externally without abandoning your core. This rhythm can be felt when you walk into a room, speak with conviction tempered by compassion, and make decisions that reflect both courage and care. It's leadership that breathes — expanding, contracting, adjusting — without breaking.

A composed leader doesn't dominate their environment; they recalibrate it. Their presence acts as a stabilizing force, not through authority but through attunement. They demonstrate a way of being that invites others into coherence. In that coherence, teams experience what true leadership truly is — not pressure from above, but alignment from within.

The Mosaic in motion represents leadership at its most human and impactful — a living example of what can happen when integrity, empathy, and identity work together in harmony.

Mosaic in Action — Leading Through Integration

During a complex merger at a multinational corporation, a regional director was tasked with uniting two teams shaped by different histories, leadership styles, and unspoken loyalties. Tension simmered beneath polite exchanges. Legacy groups sat on opposite sides of meeting rooms. Collaboration stalled, not because people lacked skill, but because they lacked safety. Every suggestion felt like a negotiation. Every initiative felt like a competition. She knew a mandate wouldn't dissolve the divide; it would only deepen it.

Instead of enforcing alignment through authority, she chose to foster integration through reflection. At each leadership meeting, she started with a simple, consistent ritual: "Share one insight you've gained from the other team this week." It wasn't a soft question; it was a strategic one. It demanded perspective-taking, emotional honesty, and mutual recognition. Initially, responses were superficial — compliments about efficiency, timelines, or communication style. But over time, the answers became more personal and vulnerable. Leaders began identifying strengths they had previously overlooked, acknowledging misunderstandings they had carried, and expressing appreciation for approaches different from their own.

By the fourth week, something remarkable occurred. The tone shifted. Competition softened into curiosity. Defensive postures transformed into mutual respect. People began partnering on projects before being asked. Meetings became less about defending legacy turf and more about shaping a shared future. Her calm didn't erase the differences; it aligned them. It allowed two distinct cultures to breathe in the same direction.

The regional director practiced the Mosaic Way™ in action. Her reflection ritual demonstrated emotional honesty (naming tension without shame), cultural adaptability (encouraging leaders to appreciate different perspectives), and identity agility (helping teams develop without losing their histories). Integration became the new measure of efficiency — not because she required unity, but because she exemplified coherence. Belonging became the new standard for success, and the merger thrived because its people embraced it.

The Advantage in a Noisy World

In a world filled with noise, calmness is the new way to stand out. Noise is reactive; true presence is rare. That rarity is what makes you memorable. The Mosaic Advantage™ isn't about louder leadership — it's about clear leadership.

True influence doesn't come from volume but from vibration. When you walk into a chaotic room and remain unshaken, you reset the emotional temperature. When you speak with measured conviction, people lean in closer. When you choose based on alignment rather than anxiety, people trust the outcome even before they understand it.

The future doesn't require faster leaders; it demands steadier ones — those who understand that calm is not passive but influential. Composure isn't withdrawal; it's authority demonstrated through awareness. In an age of overload, the clearest message will always be coherence.

The Deep Work of Integration

Integration isn't a one-time moment; it's a steady rhythm. You will lose your composure. You will forget your tools. You will fall back into old patterns of control or urgency. But growth isn't about how rarely you fall — it's about how quickly you get back up.

The true mark of Mosaic mastery is recovery speed — not perfection, but returning. The deep work of integration involves recognizing the drift without shame and reorienting without delay. It's the quiet discipline of saying, I slipped — and I can still find my way back. That's what sustainable leadership sounds like: resilience rooted in grace, practiced one return at a time.

Integration as Legacy

When your leadership is integrated, your legacy becomes less about what you built and more about how you made people feel while building it. They will remember the calm you brought into chaos, the way you created space for their voice, and the grace with which you owned your mistakes and repaired what pressure broke.

The Mosaic Advantage™ isn't just a framework you move on from — it's a mark that lingers in others. It's the emotional impact of coherence: courage, clarity, and connection. Long after your words fade, people will remember how it felt to be led by you — seen, safe, and steady. That is the quiet power of integrated presence.

Integration is not the destination; it is the doorway. From here, leadership moves beyond the individual into the collective — into classrooms, boardrooms, and communities shaped by coherence. The Epilogue turns outward, exploring how composure becomes culture and how integrated leaders seed systems of calm.

Reflection — Living the Mosaic

Pause and breathe. Ask yourself:

- Where am I most cohesive in my leadership, and where am I still divided?
- Do my words align with my energy, or do I act calm while harboring chaos?
- How can I live The Mosaic Way not just as a strategy, but as a consistent way of being?

The Mosaic Advantage isn't something you achieve once and for all — it's something you revisit repeatedly until coherence becomes your second language. Because the future will not belong to the fastest or the loudest, it will belong to the composed — those who no longer fight the storm, but have learned to embody the stillness inside it.

!

The Data That Demands Attention

Integration of language, emotion, and identity is now a measurable advantage. According to McKinsey's 2024 Future of Leadership report, leaders who demonstrate emotional intelligence, cultural awareness, and clear communication outperform peers by 45 percent in adaptive decision-making. Harvard Business Review's 2023 analysis of high-trust organizations similarly found that teams led by emotionally attuned communicators reported 76 percent higher engagement and greater innovation capacity.

Fragmentation, on the other hand, is costly. Deloitte's Global Workplace Survey showed that one in two leaders struggles with "identity dissonance"—feeling pressure to act differently in different situations—which is linked to higher turnover and lower authenticity ratings from direct reports. The expense of maintaining composure without coherence is credibility itself.

The data emphasize what the Mosaic framework has demonstrated all along: integration enhances effectiveness. When leaders align language with empathy and identity with truth, they go beyond management to influence. The mosaic, once assembled, becomes the model—proof that wholeness is a competitive advantage.

A Word to the Generations

 **Generation X** You've built your leadership on structure and consistency. Now, integration means synthesis—bringing together your experience, emotion, and insight into one conversation. That unity is your strength.

 **Millennials** You've long connected worlds—corporate and creative, digital and human. The Mosaic Advantage gives you permission to be completely multidimensional. Your wholeness is exactly what the system needs.

 **Generation Z** You embody intersectionality naturally. Guard that gift. Integration isn't about blending in; it's about functioning clearly within complexity.

 **Generation Alpha** You will never experience a world without multiple identities and expressions. Your strength will be balance—the ability to honor every part of yourself without losing your core.

 **Generation Beta** You will be multifaceted by default. Your advantage will come from integrating emotion, culture, and identity into coherent presence.

Which part of your generational voice feels strongest right now—clarity, connection, speed, or listening?

The Composed Practice

Composed — Chapter 11: The Mosaic Advantage

Integration · Alignment · Presence

I no longer perform calm — I embody it.
My language, my values, and my presence move as one.
I am not scattered between who I am and who I must be. I
am whole.

Pause here.
Feel the stillness that comes when nothing inside you is at
war.
Integration is not perfection—it is peace made visible.

You have spent years learning to manage, translate, and
adapt.
Now, composure lives in your fluency — where honesty
replaces image, and presence becomes the message.

Ask yourself, *Do my words match my energy?*
Do people feel safer after hearing me speak?

Whisper softly, *I am coherence in motion.*
Let that awareness anchor you as you lead,
reminding you that clarity is not control — it's connection.

Your composure is now your signature.
And your signature is wholeness.

CHAPTER 12 ———————————————

The Path Home

Language Cue: Wholeness
The return to yourself without losing your mission.

From Integration to Embodiment

After integration comes embodiment — the quiet phase where coherence becomes character. Integration helps you understand the rhythm of composure; embodiment helps you *inhabit* it. This is the stage where your inner alignment stops feeling like something you visit and starts feeling like somewhere you live. It is not dramatic. There is no applause, no milestone to announce. Embodiment is subtle, steady, and unmistakably powerful.

The final step of composure is not mastery; it is homecoming. You are no longer trying to "be composed." You are returning to the self that pressure once scattered — the self that can breathe before reacting, listen before defending, and choose presence over performance. Embodiment is the internal shift where the strategies you practiced become the instincts you trust.

You have already learned to regulate, repair, and realign. Now, the challenge is to live what you know. Embodiment turns calm from a concept into muscle memory, from a framework into a rhythm your body recognizes even when your mind is tired. It's the moment when composure stops being something you reach for and becomes what you return to.

In practice, leadership shifts from effort to essence. You influence not by trying harder but by being clearer. Your presence speaks louder than your words. Your steadiness guides others, and your internal coherence acts as a quiet compass they trust when uncertainty arises.

This is the maturity of composure — not a perfect state, but a practiced way of being. The work is no longer about holding it together; it is about moving through the world with the kind of grounded sincerity that makes others feel safer simply by your arrival.

The Long Way Back

Every leader eventually reaches a moment when the noise of achievement fades, and deeper questions start to surface. It happens quietly — sometimes after a milestone, sometimes after a mistake, and sometimes during the stillness between transitions. The titles, deadlines, and demands that once defined you begin to lose their importance, and a softer inquiry begins to emerge.

Who am I when the results are gone?
Who am I when the applause stops?
Who am I when the system finally quiets?

It's in this rare stillness that you realize the journey was never just about performance. It was about becoming someone worth following — someone whose presence influences more than their pressure, whose inner alignment speaks louder than their achievements, and whose integrity outlasts their accomplishments.

You've endured seasons of pressure that stretched your capacity. You've recalibrated your identity again and again as circumstances changed. You've learned to manage emotions in motion rather than deny them. You've repaired what pressure broke, restored what exhaustion blurred, and relearned the difference between composure and suppression.

And through this work, you have practiced composure not as a mask to hide fatigue, but as a mirror, reflecting your integrity back into every room you enter. Your calm no longer performs; it communicates. It steadies without hardening. It softens without collapsing.

Now, at this final turning point, the path home begins — not as an ending, but as a re-entry.

A return to the self you've been becoming along the way.

A return to the truth that leadership has always been more human than strategic.

A return to presence — not performance.

This is the long way back: back to yourself, back to coherence, and back to the kind of leadership that doesn't rely on control but is rooted in clarity. It's about understanding that the greatest leaders are not those who hold everything together, but those who remain whole even as everything around them shifts.

The long journey back shows that leadership, at its core, is not about endurance but about humanity — a steady, brave return to who you are when all the noise fades away.

The Return to Presence

Presence is both the beginning and the end of leadership. It is not something you perform; it is something you inhabit. Throughout this journey, you have built the inner architecture of composure—learning to listen to your body's signals, to language emotion with precision, and to recover rhythm after rupture. Presence begins in breath. Every inhale gathers awareness; every exhale releases control. The body becomes the bridge between intention and impact. To live from presence is to stop being divided—between what you say and what you feel, between who you are and who you think you must be. It is the seamless integration of values, voice, and visibility. When you lead from presence, people experience not your perfection but your peace. And in a culture addicted to urgency and performance, that peace becomes a form of quiet rebellion—leadership as regulation in motion.

The Wisdom of the Wound

Every Mosaic is made from what once broke. There is no leadership without fracture, no composure without repair. The very moments that once shamed you, silenced you, or stretched you beyond recognition are the same moments that now give you the empathy and depth to hold others. The path home isn't about erasing the past; it's about transforming it. The scar becomes a lesson. The failure becomes a foundation. The silence becomes understanding. Your credibility as a leader isn't measured by how little you've struggled but by how authentically you've healed. Composed leaders don't lead from invincibility; they lead from recovery. They show that resilience isn't about returning unchanged; it's about returning wiser, with compassion still intact.

The Permission to Be Human

You can stop now. You have nothing left to prove. The highest form of composure is humanity without apology. It's being able to say, "I don't know yet," without losing authority. It's laughing again after burnout. It's leading with empathy even when efficiency is easier. When you give yourself permission to be human, you give permission to everyone around you. Your honesty becomes an act of healing. Your self-compassion becomes the culture's permission to breathe. This is the core of The Mosaic Way™: leadership that doesn't create followers but restores people to themselves. True composure doesn't diminish emotion — it dignifies it.

The Mirror and the Window

Every leader must learn to navigate between two key perspectives — the mirror and the window. The mirror symbolizes reflection: looking inward to assess motives, emotions, and behaviors. The window symbolizes awareness: looking outward to understand others' needs and rhythms. Composure exists in balancing both. Too much reflection risks self-absorption, while too much outward focus causes you to lose your center. The Mosaic Leader embodies both —

mirror and window — moving smoothly between self-awareness and empathy. When you keep both perspectives in harmony, you lead with clarity and compassion. You see yourself honestly and others clearly. That balance is what it means to be truly present — grounded inwardly and attuned outwardly.

When Calm Becomes Culture

By now, you've realized that composure was never meant to be a solo effort. It's contagious. The way you regulate yourself influences the emotional environment others absorb—calm spreads through modeling, not rules. When you live The Mosaic Way™, people start to mirror it. They pause before reacting. They listen longer before responding. They lead with empathy instead of ego. Clarity replaces confusion; belonging replaces burnout. Your steadiness becomes the team's rhythm. That's how calm becomes culture — one regulated voice, one centered presence, one authentic conversation at a time. Leadership doesn't grow through slogans; it grows through state.

Mosaic in Action — A School That Breathed Again

After a turbulent semester marked by staff turnover, student behavioral spikes, and growing exhaustion among teachers, a principal realized her campus didn't need another initiative — it needed space to breathe. Meetings had become hurried, tense, and transactional, reflecting the urgency that had overtaken the school's culture. People were showing up, but no one felt truly present.

She chose to start a simple ritual: a one-minute pause. At the beginning of each staff meeting, she asked everyone to put down their laptops, silence their phones, and close their eyes if they wished. No agenda. No announcements. No motivational speeches. Just breathing. Sixty calm seconds of stillness.

Initially, the room felt awkward — a shared unfamiliarity with slowing down. But by the third week, a subtle change began. Shoulders relaxed. The energy settled. Conversations mellowed. Teachers started arriving a few minutes early, rather than rushing in at the last second. The moment of stillness became an anchor in a job usually defined by constant motion.

Within a few weeks, staff reported feeling calmer not just in meetings but also in their classrooms. They started modeling intentional breathing with students during transitions. Tense moments de-escalated more quickly. The tone in the hallways softened. Even parent conferences began to feel different. What began as a one-minute pause turned into a cultural reset—a reminder that regulation is contagious, and so is composure.

The principal hadn't introduced a program; she had introduced a presence. Her micro-practice was an expression of emotional integrity (acknowledging the school's burnout), cultural flexibility (creating space that honored the nervous systems of diverse educators), and identity agility (choosing a leadership move rooted in humanity instead of pressure). Calm became part of the school's culture because one person modeled composure as belonging, and the entire community learned to breathe again.

The Discipline of Stillness

The modern world confuses stillness with stagnation, but stillness is not the absence of motion — it is the mastery of direction. The composed leader doesn't rush to fill the silence; they let it reveal itself. They don't chase visibility; they cultivate value. Stillness is where insight matures. It is not withdrawal but awareness — the sacred pause that allows truth to surface. In stillness, you rediscover that leadership's most powerful movements begin in quiet reflection, not external noise. When you practice stillness, you reclaim authorship over your attention. You stop reacting to everything that demands urgency and start responding to what truly deserves energy. In that shift, your *Mosaic Advantage*™ — the quiet strength of coherence — becomes unmistakable.

Integration as Return

By now, The Mosaic Way™ has become more than just a framework; it has transformed into a way of life. It no longer exists outside of you as a collection of ideas to recall; it lives within you as a rhythm you embody. Emotional integrity has taught you to remain honest even when fear tempts you to perform. Cultural flexibility has shown you how to broaden your perspective without wavering in your core values. Identity agility has helped you evolve without losing your essence. Together, these qualities have guided you back to yourself — to a place where composure no longer feels like a performance, but a presence you can trust.

Integration isn't about assembling perfect pieces into a flawless whole; it's about accepting what is imperfect and finding meaning in it. It's the understanding that fractures aren't failures but teachers — signs of pressure you've endured and marks of strength you've earned. Integration enables you to hold contradictions, doubts, old identities, and new ones without falling apart. It marks the shift from asking, 'What is wrong with me?' to questioning, 'What is this part of me trying to teach?'

This kind of wholeness doesn't come from erasing the past; it comes from including it. Every version of you — the armored one, the hopeful one, the exhausted one, the resilient one — is part of your story. Integration allows each one to take its rightful place in your mosaic without overwhelming the present. It's a homecoming built on acknowledgment rather than avoidance.

You find yourself not by rejecting the chapters that were difficult, but by weaving them into a deeper truth. Integration occurs when your past ceases to be a place of judgment and becomes a place of understanding. It's where composure matures into a steady, lived rhythm — honest, human, and whole.

The Mosaic Advantage™ Revisited

The Mosaic Advantage™ is more than just a framework — it's a way of living in alignment. Its power comes from the balance of three key capacities: **emotional integrity, cultural flexibility, and identity agility.** Each one is important on its own, but together they create a leadership language that is both stabilizing and transformative. Emotional integrity keeps you grounded in truth. Cultural flexibility broadens your connection to others. Identity agility allows you to stay adaptable without losing your sense of self. When these three capacities work together, leadership feels less like performance and more like presence.

This harmony elevates composure beyond mere self-control. It becomes a way of engaging with the world with clarity and compassion. You start to speak purposefully rather than urgently, respond with curiosity rather than defensiveness, and navigate pressure with a steadiness that others can sense. The Mosaic Advantage™ shifts leadership from just a role you assume to a rhythm you live by. Presence becomes a source of peace — not only for you, but for everyone who enters your space.

At its essence, this is the architecture of wholeness. It is leadership built on coherence, where your inner world and outer impact align. It is influence rooted in compassion, where differences become bridges instead of barriers. And it is a conscious rhythm, one that lets you lead without fragmentation and connect without losing yourself. When the Mosaic Advantage™ is lived, not just understood, leadership becomes an act of integration — grounded, human, and deeply restorative.

Legacy as Continuum

The Mosaic Way™ doesn't end with you; it flows through you. Every choice you make — every moment you choose integrity over impression, clarity over control, empathy over efficiency — expands the path for someone who will follow behind you. Leadership becomes a legacy the moment your presence changes the atmosphere for others. Legacy isn't just the story you leave behind; it's the momentum you create.

Titles, outcomes, or achievements don't measure true legacy. It's measured by atmosphere. Titles expire. Achievements fade. But the emotional climate you create in rooms, teams, and relationships becomes part of the environments people carry forward. Atmospheres outlast accomplishments. Those who think of you years from now won't first recall your strategies; they'll remember how you made them feel — safer, seen, steadier, more capable, more human.

Legacy isn't about maintaining your image; it's about helping others reclaim their own. It leaves an impression of your composure on the nervous systems of those you've led. It is the steadiness they learned to adopt because they observed you breathe before reacting, listen before defending, and stand in truth without hardening. Composed leadership does not merely shape outcomes — it shapes identities.

This is the quiet revolution of composure: leadership as restoration, presence as inheritance. Your legacy is not a monument; it is a continuum. It moves through the people who witnessed your alignment, learned from your calm, and found themselves again because you modeled what it means to remain whole.

Coming Home

Coming home isn't about returning to who you once were; it's about realizing that home has always been within you. The journey you've taken through The Mosaic Way™ hasn't been a search for a new self, but a remembrance of an original one — the self beneath the striving, expectations, and noise. Every chapter has reflected you back to yourself. Each reflection has slowed you enough to hear the truth inside you that pressure once silenced.

Coming home is the moment you realize that composure wasn't something to attain; it was something to reclaim. You haven't learned how to steady your emotions — you've learned how to return to the place inside you that has always known how to breathe, listen, and lead with clarity and grace. You've remembered who you are when you're not performing, protecting, or proving. You've remembered the self that doesn't disappear under pressure but becomes more defined because of it.

That is the ultimate Mosaic Advantage™: not that you never break, but that you always rebuild — stronger in integrity, softer in compassion, and wiser in presence. Resilience isn't the absence of fracture; it's the capacity to reorganize, realign, and return. You now know how to find your center without apology, regulate without rigidity, and lead without losing your core identity.

And when the next storm arrives — which it will — remember this truth: you don't have to hold everything together. You only need to hold yourself. Your coherence is enough. Your presence is enough. Your calm is not the opposite of courage; it is evidence of it. Coming home is the moment you realize that the strength you've been seeking has been living inside your steadiness all along.

Reflection — The Path Continues

As you close this book, open your awareness. This is not an ending; it's a deep beginning. Ask yourself:

- What does "home" mean to me now?
- How will I protect my composure without losing connection?
- Where can I bring calm next — not as performance, but as presence?

The Mosaic Way will continue to evolve with you. Each act of courage, each pause of reflection, each word spoken in alignment adds another tile to the living design. You are not the same leader who began this journey. You are composed — not as control, but as connection, not as performance, but as peace.

And the world needs that version of you — the one who remembers that true leadership was never about holding power, but about holding presence.

Welcome home.

!

The Data That Demands Attention

Leaders are now judged not only by what they create but also by how they recover. The 2024 American Psychological Association report on Workplace Well-Being and Leadership Longevity showed that 68 percent of leaders identify emotional exhaustion as their biggest professional risk. However, those who deliberately practice self-renewal—through reflection, rest, or reconnection—are 50 percent more likely to maintain high performance over time.

A 2023 study by the Stanford Center for Compassion and Altruism Research found that leaders who regularly practice gratitude and reflection tend to have lower cortisol levels and higher resilience markers after organizational crises. The results suggest that recovery is both physiological and philosophical: meaning restores the body as much as it restores the mission.

As the pace of modern work speeds up, emotional sustainability has become a strategic necessity. The way home isn't about retreating from ambition — it's about restoring it. Practicing composure as renewal fosters longevity. It guarantees that leadership concludes not in depletion, but in leaving a legacy.

A Word to the Generations

 **Generation X** — You have guided through eras of disruption and change. Your wisdom now resides in teaching endurance with grace. Home, for you, is not a place—it's peace.

 **Millennials** — You have carried the vision of meaningful work through chaos and change. Let this be the decade you learn to rest without guilt. Recovery is not the end of purpose—it's what keeps it pure.

 **Generation Z** — You prioritize authenticity over approval and presence over perfection. Guard that. The journey home reminds you that emotional rest isn't rebellion — it's part of your responsibility.

 **Generation Alpha** — You will inherit a future shaped by speed. Learn to find stillness early on. The quiet you cultivate now will become the leadership others admire later.

 **Generation Beta** — You will navigate vast futures. Home will be the ability to return to yourself—again and again—without losing your way forward.

Which part of your generational voice feels strongest right now—clarity, connection, speed, or listening?

The Composed Practice

Composed — Chapter 12: The Path Home

Wholeness · Return · Peace

I am no longer seeking calm — I have become it.
Home is not a place I find; it is a presence I carry.
I lead from alignment, not exhaustion.

Breathe.
Let this breath remind you that you have nothing left to
     prove.
Leadership is not holding everything together — it is holding
     yourself with grace.

The journey has refined you.
Every fracture became a window.
Every return a reminder that strength is not resistance — it is
     restoration.

Ask yourself, *What does home feel like in me now?*
Where can I bring peace without performing it?

Whisper quietly, *I am here. I am whole. I am home.*
Let those words become your rhythm,
a composure that travels wherever you go.

Because the greatest leadership is not about reaching
     higher —
it's about returning deeper.

AFTERWORD

The Invitation

The Quiet Shift

There is always a moment, after the last chapter closes, when the reader exhales—not because the journey is over, but because something inside has quietly shifted. That is what *Composed* was meant to do—not simply to teach, but to awaken. If you've come this far, you've walked through more than a framework. You've moved through a mirror. You've examined how pressure changes you, how language shapes you, and how presence restores you. You've seen that composure isn't the art of pretending to be fine—it's the practice of remembering that you already are whole.

You've learned that leadership, at its core, is not about control—it's about clarity. And that strength, at its peak, is not about performance—it's about peace. The Mosaic Way™ starts where most leadership models end. It starts with you.

The Work Beyond the Page

Books can raise awareness, but true change happens in practice. The Mosaic Way™ was never meant to be a concept to admire; it was created as a way to live. It is for those who are done performing composure and ready to embody it—for those who want to lead without losing themselves, not by suppressing emotion, but by refining it. Each pillar—Emotional Integrity, Cultural Flexibility, and Identity

Agility—acts as both a mirror and a movement. Together, they transform chaos into coherence and reaction into rhythm.

The work beyond the page seems deceptively simple, but it is deeply demanding. Practice emotional honesty when pressure makes you want to pretend. Listen across differences when fear makes you want to defend. Allow yourself to grow when comfort makes you want to control. That's how The Mosaic Way™ moves from philosophy to freedom—not through force, but through consistent, mindful practice.

Language as Leadership

Every leader possesses a language—sometimes inherited, sometimes reactive, often unconscious. The current aim is to make that language deliberate. Language is the tool for creating composure. It transforms emotion into direction, conflict into dialogue, and chaos into coherence. That's why The Mosaic Way™ Field Glossary exists: to provide leaders with the vocabulary they've been missing—to express what pressure too often takes away.

When you can name what you feel, you can navigate what you face. When you can name what others feel, you can repair what pressure has broken. Language doesn't describe your world—it creates it. Every sentence you speak builds or destroys the emotional structure of trust. So choose words that heal, not harden. Choose tone that calms, not reacts. Choose meanings that restore, not perform. That is how you speak Mosaic—with language that makes people feel seen rather than controlled, understood rather than analyzed, and connected rather than compared.

Leadership as Art

In every generation, a new kind of leader emerges—not one who commands the room, but one who composes it. Their presence transforms chaos into calm and dissonance into direction. They are less of a conductor and more of a composer—not managing noise but creating harmony.

This is the leader the future needs: grounded, generous, and attuned. The one who leads from within, not from above. The one who listens deeply enough to influence systems from the inside out. Leadership, like art, is an expression born from coherence. When you are emotionally integrated, culturally fluent, and identity-secure, everything you touch carries that signature of wholeness. That is your Mosaic—not something you imitate, but something you become.

The Invitation Forward

If this book reached you at a crossroads—somewhere between burnout and belonging, between clarity and confusion—consider it your return ticket. The Mosaic Way™ is not a destination; it is a discipline, a rhythm you carry on long after the last page. Continue your journey through the spaces designed to deepen your fluency and support your growth.

The Mosaic Way™ Field Glossary transforms language into leadership literacy. The Mosaic Intelligence™ Puzzle Series combines reflection with play. Courses and Retreats help turn composure into culture. Each resource aims to support your journey—a community of leaders, educators, and creators who understand that what you now know is: calm is not compliance, and belonging is not a bonus. Belonging is the work, and maintaining composure is how you sustain it.

The Mosaic Promise

Every reader who finishes Composed adds another tile to the living Mosaic—a collective of leaders dedicated to emotional depth, cultural adaptability, and authentic identity. You don't need to change the world to make a difference; you only need to change the atmosphere around you.

Your calm influences the flow. Your words reshape the culture. Your presence becomes the quiet force for change. That—consistently, courageously—is how The Mosaic Way™ spreads: one grounded leader, one conversation, one moment of coherence at a time.

At the end of the book, you'll discover **The Seven-Day Practice of Composure**—a rhythm of reflection inspired by the emotional and cultural language of The Mosaic Way™. It serves as your guided return to center, crafted to help you incorporate what you've learned into your daily routine, one intentional pause at a time.

As you close this book, carry its rhythm into your next meeting, your next decision, your next day. Lead as if your presence proves possibility—because it does.

You are complete. You are whole.

You are home.

The Seven-Day Practice of Composure

A Prelude to the Work

Composure isn't a personality trait — it's a rhythm. It's the daily alignment of emotion, identity, and intention. While The Mosaic Advantage™ teaches you the principles of emotional integrity, cultural flexibility, and identity agility, this practice provides something different: an experiential approach. It shifts ideas from your mind into your nervous system, turning concepts into capacity.

This seven-day practice is not a challenge, a detox, or a performance of discipline. It is a quiet recalibration. Each day offers a single, intentional focus supported by language cues from The Mosaic Way™. These cues give your nervous system a shared vocabulary for awareness, grounding, and connection. They are not tasks to complete — they are invitations to return to yourself.

How to Use This Practice

You can treat this plan as a daily companion or as a reflection tool woven into the fabric of your week. Each day includes:

- **A focus theme** that anchors your emotional awareness
- **A guided practice** that fosters inner alignment

- **A brief reflection** that strengthens your language of composure
- **A closing cue** to integrate the lesson into action

The practice takes **5–10 minutes per day**. You don't need perfect silence or a special environment. You need willingness — the openness to pause, notice, and recalibrate without judgment.

There is no "right" way to complete this plan. You can:

- follow the days in order,
- repeat a single day for as long as needed,
- or pair the practice with moments that naturally arise in your leadership rhythm: after meetings, before hard conversations, or at the beginning or end of your day.

How Often to Use It

Treat this seven-day framework as a **repeatable cycle**, not a one-time event. Many readers return to it:

- **Weekly**, as a grounding rhythm
- **Monthly**, as a leadership reset
- **Quarterly**, as part of strategic planning
- **Whenever pressure increases**, as a personal recalibration

The more consistently you engage, the faster your nervous system learns the rhythm of composure as a familiar state, not an occasional experience.

What to Expect: The Impact of the Practice

Consistent use of this seven-day rhythm builds three key outcomes:

1. Emotional Clarity
You become more fluent in naming what you feel before it becomes noise, reactivity, or withdrawal.

2. Nervous System Stability

Composure becomes embodied — not an idea, but a physiological experience you can access on demand.

3. Leadership Presence

Your tone softens, your decisions sharpen, and your relationships deepen.

People trust leaders who can return to themselves quickly.

Over time, you'll notice subtle but profound shifts:

- You pause more easily.
- You interpret emotion instead of absorbing it.
- You set boundaries without guilt.
- You repair relationships more quickly.
- You lead with presence instead of performance.

This is the Mosaic Advantage™ in motion — composure as a daily practice, not a distant ideal.

The Seven-Day Practice of Composure

A rhythm of reflection drawn from the emotional and cultural language of The Mosaic Way™

Day 1 – Return to Integrity

Focus: Emotional Honesty

Begin with truth. Before you enter the day's conversations, pause and ask yourself: *What am I actually feeling right now?* Not what you should feel. Not what is expected of you. What is real? Emotional integrity begins with self-recognition. When you can tell the truth to yourself, your leadership naturally becomes more trustworthy.

Practice:

Take five quiet minutes. Name three emotions you've been carrying this week. Beside each one, write what it might be trying to teach you. End with a grounding phrase — something simple, like *"I can breathe here."* Let this become the anchor of your calm today.

Day 2 – Reclaim Your Rhythm

Focus: Regulation

Composure isn't the absence of feeling; it's the mastery of rhythm. When your nervous system steadies, your presence steadies others. Notice how your body signals stress—shallow breathing, tightened shoulders, scattered thoughts. These are invitations, not interruptions.

Practice:

Inhale for four counts, hold for two, and exhale for six. Repeat this rhythm three times before your next meeting or meaningful conversation. Each exhale signals to your body that safety has returned.

Day 3 – Listen Across Difference

Focus: Cultural Flexibility

Practice curiosity over certainty. When someone's tone, language, or worldview challenges you, resist the urge to defend or correct. Ask instead: *What are they trying to protect or express?* Cultural flexibility is not agreement; it is expanded awareness.

Practice:

In your next conversation, listen for the meaning beneath their method of communication. Afterwards, write one sentence about what you learned from that person's perspective. Let curiosity replace conclusion.

Day 4 – Anchor in Identity

Focus: Identity Agility

Leadership often tempts you to perform rather than be. Identity agility invites you to adapt without abandoning yourself. Remember: who you are is not your role; it is your rhythm.

Practice:

At the end of the day, ask: *Where did I lead from essence instead of ego?* Write one moment where you stayed aligned with your values even when outcomes shifted. That is the quiet evidence of integrity in motion.

Day 5 – Speak with Intention

Focus: Language and Tone

Your words are instruments of regulation. Before you speak, ask: *Will this language build trust or tension?* Composure is audible — it lives in tone, pace, and precision.

Practice:

Choose one emotionally charged phrase from your week — something you wish had landed differently. Rewrite it through the lens of composure. How could you express the same truth with more clarity, grace, and steadiness?

Day 6 – Create Restorative Space

Focus: Containment

Every system needs a container strong enough to hold emotion without collapsing. Boundaries are not distance; they are design. Rest today from constant availability. Let silence become structure.

Practice:

Identify one space — mental, physical, or relational — that needs pause. Set a gentle boundary: *"I'll respond after I rest,"* or *"Let's revisit this tomorrow."* Notice how clarity becomes a source of calm.

Day 7 – Embody Wholeness

Focus: Integration

You've practiced emotional integrity, regulation, cultural flexibility, and reflective presence. Today, practice integration — allowing them to move as one. Wholeness is not perfection; it is coherence. It is when your emotions, language, and leadership presence share the same rhythm.

Practice:

Take a walk or sit in quiet stillness. Reflect on this question: *Where did I feel most like myself this week?* That moment of alignment is your compass. Let it guide how you step into the week ahead.

The Rhythm Continues

Composure is not a one-time achievement — it is a daily return.
These seven days are not a checklist but a cycle.
Begin again whenever pressure fractures your peace.
Each return strengthens your rhythm.

Each return sharpens your leadership.

Each return brings you closer to yourself.

The Mosaic Way™ will meet you there — not as performance, but as presence.

The Mosaic Way™ Field Glossary

Lead with Language. Shape Culture. Create Belonging.

Before culture shifts, language shifts. Before belonging grows, it must be spoken into being.

Across boardrooms, classrooms, and communities, the words we choose shape the culture we create. The *Mosaic Way™ Field Glossary* was designed for leaders, educators, innovators, and changemakers who understand that inclusive leadership begins with the language we use every day.

More than a dictionary, this glossary is a living leadership companion—a guide to identity-aware, culturally intelligent, emotionally attuned communication. Rooted in The Mosaic Intelligence Method™, it gives you the vocabulary, insight, and awareness to bridge differences, build trust, and lead with empathy.

Every entry invites you to consider how language shapes perception, power, and belonging. It redefines what it means to "speak like a leader" in a world where influence is measured not only by strategy but by sensitivity, resonance, and human understanding.

Inside, you'll find:

1,000 enhanced definitions with real-world leadership, business, and education applications

Cultural cautions that illuminate blind spots and deepen cross-cultural intelligence

Leadership insights that translate emotional literacy into everyday practice

Mosaic Questions™ that open meaningful dialogue and expand perspective

Each definition goes beyond terminology—it reveals how words carry history, emotion, identity, and context. Whether you are leading a diverse team, teaching across cultures, navigating difficult conversations, or building the foundations of an inclusive culture, you'll find language that supports clarity, courage, and connection.

This is not a reference book—it is a movement in print. The *Mosaic Way*™ *Field Glossary* equips you with tools to refine your communication, rethink assumptions, and reimagine what belonging can look like in action.

Perfect for:

- Leaders guiding diverse or global teams
- Educators creating inclusive learning spaces
- Coaches and facilitators designing development programs
- Organizations committed to equity, belonging, and cultural intelligence

In a world where words can wound or repair, divide or unite, the leaders who master the language of belonging will shape the future. This glossary helps you do exactly that—offering vocabulary and wisdom you can apply immediately.

From one-on-one conversations to international collaborations, you will gain a new fluency in the language of trust, empathy, and influence. The *Mosaic Way*™ *Field Glossary* meets you where you are and equips you to speak across difference, navigate nuance, and lead with humanity.

Wherever you lead—whether in a boardroom, classroom, nonprofit, or global context—this resource strengthens how you communicate with intention and anchor conversations that create culture.

Lead with language. Shape culture. Create belonging.

REFERENCES

American Psychological Association. *Work and Well-Being Survey: Stress and Performance Trends*. APA, 2024.

Deloitte. *Workplace Trends Report: Emotional Depletion in Modern Leadership*. Deloitte Insights, 2024.

Gallup. *State of the Global Workplace 2023 Report*. Gallup, 2023.

Gallup. *Global Emotions Report: Daily Stress Trends*. Gallup, 2024.

Gottman Institute. *Repair and Relational Dynamics: Research Summary on Conflict Recovery*. Gottman Institute, 2023.

Harvard Business Review. "Emotional Clarity as a Driver of Team Performance." *Harvard Business Review*, 2024.

Harvard Business School. *Leadership and Well-Being Index: Boundary Clarity and Productivity*. Harvard Business School Publishing, 2024.

Korn Ferry Institute. *Leadership in Transition: Emotional Expression and Retention*. Korn Ferry, 2023.

McKinsey & Company. "Leading Across Differences: Cultural and Identity Fluency in Organizations." *McKinsey Global Institute*, 2024.

McKinsey & Company. "Boundary Setting and Emotional Labor: Insights from the 2024 Workplace Survey." McKinsey & Company, 2024.

MIT Sloan Management Review. "How Leaders Repair Trust After Conflict: The Role of Timely Repair." *MIT Sloan Management Review*, 2024.

MIT Sloan Management Review. "Authenticity, Innovation, and Identity-Based Leadership." *MIT Sloan Management Review*, 2023.

Pew Research Center. *Identity and Work: How Professionals Redefined Their Personal and Professional Roles, 2019–2024*. Pew Research Center, 2024.

Surgeon General of the United States. *Workplace Burnout Advisory: A Public Health Crisis*. U.S. Department of Health and Human Services, 2023.

World Economic Forum. *Future of Jobs Report 2025*. World Economic Forum, 2025.

World Health Organization. *Mental Health and Workplace Stress: Identity Strain as an Emerging Risk Factor*. WHO, 2024.

ABOUT THE AUTHOR ———————————

Dr. **Karissa Thomas** is an award-winning author, leadership strategist, and founder of *The Mosaic Way*™ — a global framework that equips leaders to communicate, connect, and compose themselves under pressure. Her work integrates emotional intelligence, cultural agility, and identity-centered leadership into what she calls *The Mosaic Advantage*™: the ability to lead without losing yourself.

Dr. Thomas has guided thousands of professionals, educators, and executives through high-stakes transitions and organizational change. Her background spans Fortune 500 account management, international education, and crisis communication leadership — experiences that inform her belief that composure is not a personality trait, but a practiced discipline.

Her research on identity development and belonging among Western educators in the Middle East shaped the foundation of *The Mosaic Intelligence Method*™, a framework now used in leadership development, teacher training, and corporate resilience programs around the world.

Dr. Thomas is also the author of *The Mosaic Way*™ *Field Glossary*, *Lead Anyway: Teaching Through the Fog When the System Stops Seeing You*, and the *Mosaic Intelligence*™ *Puzzle Series* — a collection of tools designed to make emotional intelligence practical, teachable, and culturally relevant.

Known for her reflective storytelling and calm authority, Dr. Thomas helps leaders reclaim what pressure erodes: presence, empathy, and trust. Through her books, courses, and speaking engagements, she continues to redefine what modern composure looks like — not control, but coherence; not perfection, but presence.

To learn more or connect for speaking, training, or collaborations, visit **themosaicleader.com**.